I Made It

Exie L. Smith

Copyright © 2024 Exie L. Smith
All rights reserved
First Edition

Fulton Books
Meadville, PA

Published by Fulton Books 2024

ISBN 978-1-63985-780-7 (paperback)
ISBN 978-1-63985-781-4 (digital)

Printed in the United States of America

Contents

Introduction v

School Song 1
Segregation 3
Rosa Parks 15
Dr. Martin Luther King 17
Civil Rights Movement 19
Ku Klux Klan 21
Jim Crow Law 23
Determined to Make It 25
The Brown Decision 27
Mother 31
The Supreme Court 33
Goals in Life 35
Transition 39
Remedy of God 41
Hollywood Baptist Church 43
Radio 45
Sermons 47
Be Prepared 57
Opposite to the Devil 63
The Surrendered Life 67

There Is Power in Tears	71
Touching God through Prayer	77
Except a Man Be Born Again	81
Standing on the Rock	87
Waiting on God	93
No Easy Road to Walk	97
Strange Running Buddies	105
Depending on Jesus	113
The Price Is Right	117
If It's Not One Thing, It's Another	125
Christ's Constraineth Love	131
Coke Is the Real Thing	139
If You Need It, God Got It	145
My Grace Is Sufficient	151
Seven-ups	159
How Can the Ship Go Down When the Lord Is on Board?	163
Passport to Heaven	171
Certificates	177

INTRODUCTION

Exie L. Smith was born in Montgomery, Alabama. She attended both elementary and high school at the George Washington Carver High School in an attempt to provide for the educational, vocational, and spiritual needs of the school. Mr. W. E. Thompson was the principal.

Walking to school every day with her brothers was not a great journey. Every day, they were followed by White boys, calling them the *nigger* word.

Many times, she would cry and wonder why there was so much hatred for being a Colored person. She was taught by her mother to love everybody: the police, Asians, Jews, and so forth, regardless of a person's status.

School Song

I

Carver High, our Alma Mater
Your true love we'll share
Sons and daughters of tomorrow
ideas bright and fair.

II

Alma Mater, Alma Mater
We proudly hail thy name
Sacred walls and spacious campus
Through thy halls we came.

Chorus

Cheer, then cheer again, for Carver
Thee we'll never forget
Joy, oh joyous moments, sweet
Whenever thee we greet.

SEGREGATION

By the grace of God,
I am what I am. God gives by His grace; He saves
and protects by His grace.

We are still depending
on the blessings of God, His Spirit.

Neither He that planteth is anything, neither He
that watereth, but God gives the increase. I have tried
to love other people; I have given away many things like
money, jewelry, clothes and have shown and cared for others.

Many times she has been hurt, and others have shown
their negative part of unappreciated

for what she has given or
done for them. Finally, she turned
it over to Jesus; I knew that Jesus would
fit it.
She turned it over to Jesus;

She dried up her tears and turned
it over to Jesus.
Turn it over to Jesus. Jesus will work it
out. Turn it over to Jesus when I think about
the goodness of Jesus and all that He has
done for me, saved, healed, and delivered me.

She gets the glory, knowing that God cares for his children
and will work it out.
When a child or an adult swallows something that is poison, many times the doctor has to pump his stomach out to relieve him of that poison. All you need
to do is just turn it over to Jesus. Man has swallowed
something that has poisoned his mind. Dr. Jesus stands
ready to pump out that
hellish heart of jealousy, hated malice, and strife.

Then go down to God's surgery room, get on the table of
justification, and ask God to create in you a clean heart
and renew a right spirit within you.

We live in a sick world,
many people with a bad heart. The world is in the hospital
of sin, and the only way to get out is to look to the hills from
whence cometh your help and ask God, the Father, to
sign you out.

In August, a huge hopeful crowd of 250,000 Blacks and
Whites marched on Washington to show support for
the proposed bill.

I MADE IT

Martin Luther King Jr. addressed the crowd from
the front of the Lincoln Memorial.
The success of 1963, he said, was not an end but a beginning.

"There will be neither rest nor tranquility to America until
    the Negro is granted his citizenship rights!

We will not be satisfied until justice rolls down
like water and righteousness like a mighty stream."

The crowd cheered in jubilation as King's speech came to
    a close.

When we allow freedom to ring, when we let it ring from
    every village and
and every hamlet, from every state and city, we will be
able to speed up that day when all of God's children,

Black men and White men, Jews and Gentiles, Catholics
    and Protestants, will be able to join hands and sing in

the words of the old Negro spiritual, "Free at last, free
at last! Thank God Almighty, we are free at last! Thank
    God almighty, we are free
at last!"

Dr. King's "I Have a Dream"
speech would be remembered
as a high point of the civil
rights movement. He could have

resigned under the pressure
and despair, but he proclaimed
the conviction, the conviction
of his Black voting became
a crucial goal of the civil
rights, he said, that we shall
overcome, we shall overcome
someday. He knew that a highly
publicized integration campaign
would not sustain the movement
only by building significant
voting strength.

The civil rights movement
ended legal apartheid in
the South and forever
changed relations between
Blacks and Whites. It
continues today in the
battle against inequalities
and injustices that remain.

The spill of human blood throughout the world is
falling like rain. The only hope of this world is for us to
return to Christ.

My hope is built on nothing
less than Jesus's blood and righteousness
she dare not trust the sweetest
frame, but wholly lean on Jesus's name.

When darkness veils his lovely
face, she rests on his unchanging
grace; in every high and stormy
gale, her anchor holds within
the veil.

Blacks in America are still more likely than Whites to die in infancy, live in poverty, and drop out of school. Just hold on, hold on to God's unchanging hand.

Blacks earn less money than Whites and work at lower-skilled jobs.

Most live in segregated neighborhoods, and many still attend schools that are poorer and predominately Black.

The evidence is overwhelming that Blacks and Whites do not have equal chances in America.

The most degrading structures of discrimination brought down many of the attitudes that supported those structures still exist. Those attitudes are seen, seen in the vandalism and attacks that victimize minorities each year. They are advertised by the thousands of young neo-Nazi skinheads who listen to racist rock music, brand themselves with swastikas, and breast about bashing minorities, and they are seen daily in racial slurs, scrawled on school lockers, or shouted on school lockers or on football games.

As long as inequalities and racial prejudices remain, the work of the civil rights movement will not be finished. But we know it can be accomplished because the civil rights movement of the past proved that ordinary people can change their world. The victories of the movement were won by a largely anonymous mass of citizens, Black and White, many of them happening young, who dared to risk life and limb for freedom's cause.

Strange things are happening all over this world. If you read the newspaper, it's full of excitement.

If you watch TV or listen to the radio, all you can see and hear is fighting and riots—in the home, on the streets, in the schools and universities. When we come out of trials and tribulations, we can sing one song. We are marching up to Zion, that beautiful city of God. We can sing a charge to keep I have and a God to glorify. Every dying soul to save, fitted for the sky. Through many dangerous toils and snares, I have already come. It was Grace's will to lead me on. One day, one day, one day in God's kingdom will pay for it all.

Their hearts are full of strife. People are doing everything they are big enough to do. There is nothing too low-down or dirty for people to do.

This is a "no harm" age. There are people with a sick mind and a bad heart. She used to trick-or-treat on Halloween, but her parents stopped her from trick-or-treating on Halloween because the same people on Halloween night would put pins, needles, razor blades, and dope into children's candies and apples. A man or woman who will do a thing like that is sick with a bad heart. She woke up this morning with her mind on Jesus to live right and to love her enemies. God is good and is good all the time.

The heart is the physical center of the body, the source of life and health; when the heart is bad, it makes the whole body sick. It slows your pace to walk or run because of a bad heart. Sometimes, it will cause swelling in the feet and legs. Water will come into the veins, and if the doctor is not able to get it out, sometimes, it will overflow that bad heart.

David said that he would praise thee, O Lord, with his whole heart and that he would show forth all thy marvelous work. In Psalm 23, David said, "The Lord is my Shepherd. I shall not want, He maketh me to lie down in green pastures, He leadeth me beside the still waters, He restoreth my soul. He leadeth me in the paths of righteousness for His name's sake." But one day, David saw Urice's wife taking a bath. He had Urice put on the battlefront to be killed so he could get his wife.

David had a bad heart. Now we hear him saying, "Hide thy face from my sins, and blot out all mine iniquities. Create in me a clean heart, O God, and renew a right spirit within me."

Men are transplanting hearts. The devil is not able to transplant hearts, although the devil plants evil in the heart. He started it with Eve and Adam; the devil planted evil thoughts. Job's wife, Jonia, had a bad heart, trying to run away from God.

The world has a nervous breakdown.

The world needs to see Dr. Jesus. Let Jesus give you this prescription: a tablespoon of love three times a day. Jesus said, "Love ye one another." Let Jesus message your heart with prayer every hour of the day. Man and woman should always pray. Take a pill of faith, hope, and charity. Prayer is the key to the kingdom, but faith unlocks the door.

When a child or an adult swallows something that is poison, many times the doctor has to pump his stomach out to relieve them of that poison.

Man has swallowed something that has poisoned his mind. Dr. Jesus stands ready to pump out that hellish heart of jealousy, hate, malice, and strife. Next thing to do is to go down to God's surgery room, get on the table of justification, then ask God to create in you a clean heart and renew a right spirit with you.

David found out that he had a sick mind and a bad heart when he had Urice put on the battlefront. David began to look back and see how wrong he was. Psalm 130 says, "Out of the depths have I cried unto thee, O Lord, Lord, hear my voice: let thine ears be attentive to the voice of my supplications." In Psalm 130, David said, "Lord, my heart is not haughty, nor mine eye lofty, neither do I exercise myself in great matters, or in things too high for me." Psalm 121 says, "I will lift my mine eyes unto the hills from whence cometh my help. My help cometh from the Lord which made heaven and earth."

She is sure that God will tell man that he has taken an overdose of sin and is running a temperature of evil. Man's blood pressure is higher than it has ever been. The world has a nervous breakdown; people are afraid to walk the streets day or night. People are afraid in their homes or businesses; people are afraid to drive their own cars or ride the train or airplane. Bomb threats are everywhere. This is a sick world with a bad heart. That Great God of ours, having finished the creation of the world and all it contains, assembled a council of the Great God, Head, the Father, the Son, and the Holy Ghost: "Let us make man." From the dust of the earth, man was formed and lay there inanimate and inactive until God Almighty breathed a portion of himself (the breath of life) into man, and man arose from that earth from which he had been formed. As time winged itself by, man realized that something was missing in his life. There was a certain loneliness that ate away at the cockles of his heart.

God knows just what it was that caused man to feel so alone and incomplete; man needed a helpmate, he needed a company keeper, he needed a woman in his life. God anesthetized man and took a rib from man's side.

He took a rib from the man's side. He didn't take a bone from a man's foot because he never intended a woman to be a man's footstool. He didn't take a bone from a man's skull, for God did not intend for a woman to go ahead of a man.

But God intended for that Great God of heaven, who is wisdom, to take a bone from man's side, out of which he made a woman. God intended that in all of life's turmoils, problems, griefs and woes, trials and tribulations, yes, in all the vicissitudes of life's journey, God intended that man and woman would face them together side by side.

Equal opportunity and equal responsibility.

Yes, what the world needs is that man and woman would realize their potential in working together, unitedly, walking together, working together, loving together, praying together, and above all, staying together.

Man needed woman, and woman needed man.

God loves all of us; it doesn't matter what color you are. We were all created equal. We live in a world today that is fraught with chaos and confusion. A world of strife and turmoil. A world full of hate, envy, prejudice, and apostasy.

A world of segregation against minorities. A world in which man's inhumanity to man has reached alarming proportions.

What the world does not need at this time is divisiveness between the sexes.

"Together, we will stand, but divided, we will fall." The key to world order and what the world needs now is less thinking of self and more thinking of others.

What this old world needs to know is for men and women to realize that love is stronger than hate. It needs to learn that we are not only to love our friends who love us, but also we are to love our enemies who hate us. The world needs us to adopt this motto: "As ye would that men and women should do unto you, do ye even so to them." What this world needs now is love, sweet love.

Jesus knew that this world was not an easy life. He knew that this was not an easy life with him.

Life is toilsome and wearisome. Sometimes, Jesus wants us to realize our weaknesses and infirmities.

Learn to have faith and trust in his promises.

Our faith depends entirely on our knowing God. Faith will encourage us to base our prayers at their full-face worthwhile value when one has lost confidence in himself when there is no exemption from dangers and temptation.

Still have faith in Jesus when there is no exemption from sorrow and sins. Still have faith in Jesus if you need a million examples to justify your faith. (You don't have any faith.)

It only takes three things to justify us: faith, trust, and living Christlike. The absence of faith leaves the heart desolated; without faith in Jesus, we lose strength for life. Without faith in Jesus, we cannot force—God the conflicts of life. Without faith in Jesus, we cannot endure suffering, or with faith, the ship will not go down because Jesus is onboard.

We walk by faith and not by sight. Why are we so fearful? Jesus is the same today, yesterday, and forever. It's a little harder to calm a troubling heart than it is to calm the sea. The sea can be calm with one word from God.

It takes faith to calm a troubling heart. As long as you have faith, you are not afraid. When doubt comes in, then you will fail. Faith makes you calm as a serene chill resting in his mother's bosom. Expect no harm. In Jesus's arms, we can rest in serenity and calmness.

Whenever your storms rise in life, call the master Jesus. She was in a storm; the White boys called her names like *nigga* and threw objects at her. She was in a storm of hatred.

When she called on Jesus, he came and weathered the angry storm.

If it's troubles, call the master; if it's brokenheartedness, call the master; if it's some embarrassment, call the master; if it's sickness, call the master. If it's a weakness, call the master. Many times, I cried; she had to call on the master. God would tell the storm, "Peace, be still." After Jesus's death on the cross, He declared that all power is in His hand. I said, "My peace I give, and my peace I'll leave with you."

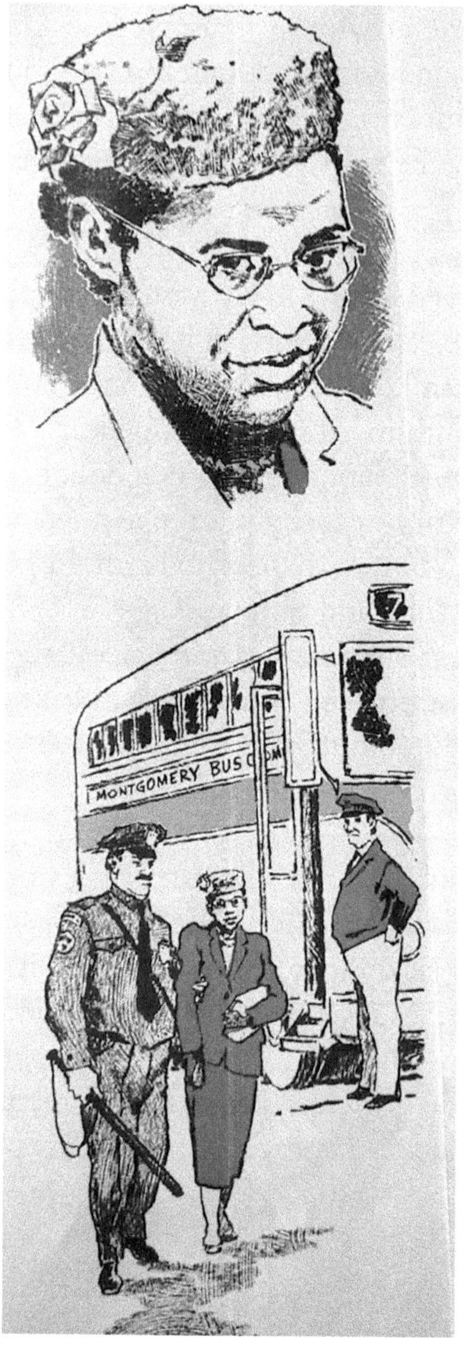
MONTGOMERY BUS

Rosa Parks

On December 1, 1955, Rosa Parks was riding home from her job as a department store seamstress.

The bus was full when a White man boarded the bus. The bus driver stopped the bus and ordered Mrs. Rosa Parks, along with three other Blacks, to vacate a row so the White man could sit down.

Three Black women stood up. Rosa Parks kept her seat and was arrested.

Joan Robinson and the women's political council began to organize a bus boycott with the support of NAACP leader E. D. Nixon.

Her mother, Mamie, and other women formed the Montgomery Improvement Association and selected a newcomer in town. Children had to attend schools that operated on one-fourth of the amount of money given to White schools. Black protests against segregation also occurred, which had been voiced for centuries.

Dr Martin King

Dr. Martin Luther King

A large crowd of fifteen thousand gathered at Holt Street church to hear the young preacher speak.

"There comes a time that people get tired," Dr. King told the crowd. "We are here this evening to say to those who have mistreated the Blacks so long that we are tired.

"Tired of being segregated and humiliated, tired of being kicked about by the brutal feet of oppression.

"We must protest. God created all of us equal. If we are wrong, the Supreme Court of this nation is wrong.

"If we are wrong, God Almighty is wrong."

Dr. King stated that if the bus boycott would be peaceful and guided by love, justice would be won.

Black people did not ride buses for 381 days in Montgomery, Alabama.

They organized carpools, walked long distances, and remained nonviolent. Even leaders were opposed to segregation.

The movement of the Blacks working together made a change.

Every day, Black housekeepers rode all the way home after work, jammed together in the aisles, while ten rows of White seats remained empty.

The Blacks could shut down the city bus systems if they wanted to.

The Black people were arranging with neighbors and friends to ride to keep them from being insulted and humiliated by bus drivers.

The mayor stated that segregation was the law, and he could not change it.

It demonstrated that poor and middle-class Blacks could unite to launch a successful protest or movement, overcoming both official counter and racist terror attacks.

Civil Rights Movement

Dr. Martin Luther King issued a nationwide appeal for support for voting.

Thousands of people came from all over the country to join in the march to Montgomery. On March 25, after four days of walking, a huge crowd gathered at the state capital. King spoke to the people about the importance of being able to vote. The Civil Rights Act of 1964 gave the Negroes some part of their rightful dignity. Without the vote, it was dignity without strength. We are still in for a season of suffering. King warned the people that violence would not stop the movement. He told the people, "Move with pride and don't give up. We must keep going." Later that day, Viola Gregg Laryzo was shot and killed by Klansmen as she was helping to transport Selma marchers. In response to the Selma march and the murders of Jackson, Reek, and Liuzzo, congress passed the Voting Rights Act on July 9, 1965. The bill outlawed obstacles to Black voting and authorized federal officials to enforce fair voting practices all over the South; thousands of Blacks were registered to vote the next year.

The Civil Rights Movement ended legal apartheid in the South and forever changed relations between Blacks and Whites. It continues today in the battle against inequalities and injustices that remain.

Black voting became a crucial goal of the Civil Rights Movement. Civil Rights activists knew that a few highly publicized integration campaigns would not sustain the movement. Only by building significant voting strength would Southern Blacks be able to keep pressure on the government to protect their rights. It was a long uphill battle against a harsh set of obstacles.

Many Blacks were afraid of reprisals or were intimidated by the complicated requirements. The movement gave Black people throughout America a renewed pride. They had forced the federal government to recognize its responsibilities. They had established their own political strength. They had seen the rise of powerful Black leaders. They had witnessed harsh rules dismantled by the courageous acts of ordinary people like themselves. Some of the younger Civil Rights activists criticized Martin Luther King Jr. for devoting resources to mass marches instead of grassroots political organizing. Some people questioned the doctrine of nonviolence, and others objected to the role played by Whites in the movement and said Blacks should build their own independent political structures.

Ku Klux Klan

Most Southern Whites were determined to keep Blacks poor, uneducated, and powerless.

The Ku Klux Klan was formed by a group of Confederate Army veterans to reestablish the reign of White supremacy.

They tried to integrate schools and other public facilities; Blacks discovered the lengths to which Whites would go to preserve White supremacy.

All over the country, Black students and parents were angered over the condition of their schools. Enough was enough. I wanted people of all races to get along. We are to love one another. What does a man profit if he shall gain the whole world and lose his own soul?

Let the wicked forsake his way, the unrighteous man his way, thoughts let him return unto the Lord, and He will have mercy upon him.

Jim Crow Law

Early one Sunday morning, dynamite bombs ripped through four churches; several homes belonging to ministers were destroyed.

I observed a fifteen-year-old Black girl who was walking to school. She was mobbed, beaten, spit upon, and cursed by a group of angry White boys.

I ran to school and told the principal what I saw. Finally, they relocated the girl and gave her medical help. I was determined to walk by faith and not by sight. The Klansmen were evil and bad, and they hated the Black people. The Jim Crow Law was on the Whites' side. But I was on the Lord's side. I was not going to give up or throw in the towel. I had come too far to turn back. I was determined to make it by the grace of God.

Determined to Make It

She was determined to strive and run that old, rugged race, and she knew life would be harder for her.

"But with Jesus, she could make it. The Lord is my light and my salvation; whom shall I fear?"

"The Lord is the strength of my life; of whom shall I be afraid, when the wicked, even my enemies, and my foes, came upon me to eat up my flesh they stumbled and fell. Though a host should encamp against me, my heart shall not fear; though war and trouble should rise against me, one thing have I desired of the Lord, all the days of my life to behold the glory and beauty of the Lord, that l will inquire in his temple. For in the time of trouble, he shall hide me in his pavilion; in the secret of his tabernacle shall he hide me; he shall set me upon a rock. And now shall mine head be lifted above mine enemies round about me: I offer in his tabernacle sacrifices of joy. I will sing, I will sing praises unto the Lord."

The Brown Decision

The *Brown v. Board of Education* ruling enraged many Southern Whites who did not believe Blacks deserved the same education as Whites.

White people didn't want their children attending schools with Black children.

Southern governors announced they would not follow the court's ruling, and White citizen councils were organized to oppose school integration.

A declaration called the Southern Manifesto was issued by ninety-six Southern congressmen demanding that the court should reverse the Brown decision.

The Brown decision gave great hope to Blacks. "With All Deliberate Speed." Black Americans knew that times were changing.

Four days after the Supreme Court handed down the Brown ruling, Mrs. Jo Ann Robinson, as president of the women's political council, wrote a letter to the mayor of Montgomery, Alabama.

She represented a large group of Black women; she only wanted fair treatment on city buses.

Blacks, who made up 75 percent of Montgomery's bus riders, were forced to enter the buses in front, pay the driver, and reenter the bus from the rear, where they could only sit in designated "Colored" seats. For 381 days, Black people did not ride the buses in Montgomery, Alabama.

If all the White seats were filled, Blacks had to give up their seats.

Those who challenged the bus drivers were stopped and beaten.

The hopes of Black Americans everywhere were hanging on the Supreme Court's decision in *the Brown v. Board of Education* case.

All men are supposed to be citizens of a country founded on the principle that all men are created equal.

Despite the opposition by many Whites, the Brown decision gave great hope to Blacks.

Even when the Supreme Court refused to order immediate integration, they were "calling instead for schools to act, with all deliberate speed."

Black Americans knew that times were changing. And they were eager for expanded rights in other areas as well.

This was just the beginning. People all across the country began to protest against unfair laws and practices. Dr. King became the best leader who knew how to show love, peace, and justice for all races. Dr. King worked hard not just for Black people but for all of God's people. Many people admired Dr. King's courage and the way he showed love for all.

The Blacks were treated unequally and declared unequal.

She kept standing and standing on the Lord, not knowing how she was going to get through the storm and the roaring wind.

She kept standing, knowing that Satan wasn't going to stop hurting her; she knew that God was her salvation.

She would trust in God and not be afraid. The Whites would call her a nigger Black girl; she learned to hold her head up high because the Lord Jehovah is her strength and becomes her salvation. Thanks be to God, who giveth us the victory through our Lord Jesus Christ.

Whatsoever is born of God overcometh the world, and she knew that this is the victory that overcometh this world, even our faith.

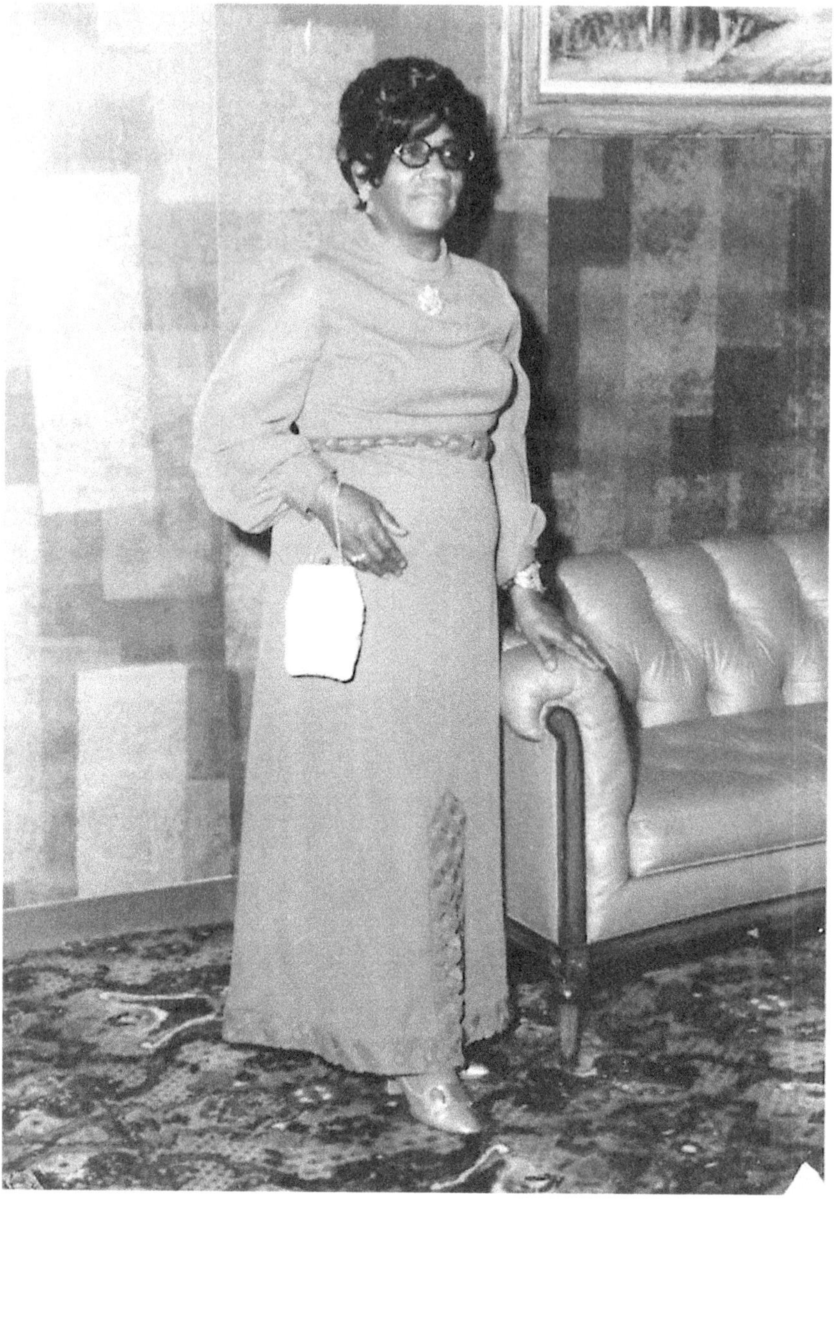

Mother

Her mother, Mamie Luckie, was called by God to preach the Word, be instant in season, reprove, and rebuke with all long-suffering and doctrine. I've seen the lightning flashing and heard the thunder roll. I've felt sin's breakers dashing, trying to conquer my soul; I've heard the voice of Jesus telling me still to fight on. He promised to never leave me, never to leave me alone.

Jesus died for me on the cross. For me, they pierced his side. For me, he opened that fountain, the crimson, cleansing tide. For me, he's waiting in glory, seated upon His throne. He promised never to leave me, never to leave me alone.

Mother maketh herself of tapestry; her clothing is silk and purple. She maketh fine linen and sellith it. She delivereth girdles unto the merchant. Strength and honor are her clothing. She shall rejoice in time to come. She openeth her mouth with wisdom, and her tongue is the law of kindness.

She looketh well to the ways of her household and eateth not the bread of idleness. Her children arise up and call her blessed; praise the Lord, and give thanks to the Lord, for He is good. Give her the fruit of her hands; let her own work praise God at the gates.

    She has fought a good fight. She finished the course, and she kept her faith in Jesus Christ.

The Supreme Court

The Whites harassed and angrily beat the Blacks.

Dr. King's home was bombed; the Black people were more determined to fight for equal justice.

The city officials tried to outlaw the boycott; the buses still traveled empty.

The Blacks were determined to work together by staying off the buses. They walked peacefully and joyfully because they knew that all things work together for good to those who love God and to those who are called according to His purpose.

On December 21, 1956, Blacks returned to the buses in triumph; the United States Supreme Court outlawed bus segregation in Montgomery, Alabama, in response to a lawsuit that was brought by the boycotters with the help of the NAACP.

It showed the world that nonviolent resistance could work.

The Blacks finally took a seat in the front of the bus after the Supreme Court ruled bus segregation was illegal.

Dr. Martin L. King continued to establish an organization of Black clergy called the Southern Christians.

Black Southern ministers tried to follow the examples of Dr. King in Montgomery and became the spiritual force behind the nonviolent movement.

If the bus boycott was peaceful and guided by love, King said, justice would be won. King predicted he would have to pause and say there lived great people, Black people, who injected new meaning and dignity into the veins of civilization. Some communities filled in their public swimming pools and closed their tennis courts, and others removed library seats rather than letting Blacks and Whites share the facilities. Blacks who challenged segregation received little help from the government.

Goals in Life

Elementary and George Washington High School

Alabama State University

Her grandfather asked her mother if her children could pick cotton.

Her grandfather had plenty of acres of land with cotton.

When the cotton grew tall and ready to be picked, her grandfather wanted the children to start right away.

When her mother told her that she was going to pick cotton with her brothers, she said yes. She always obeyed her mother's rules. She loved and cared a lot for her mother. She and her brothers went to pick cotton. She was given a long cotton bag to put the cotton in.

Instead of picking the cotton from the cone, she picked the cotton and cone together, which was the wrong way.

When the bag was full, she took it to the cotton station to be measured and checked for completion.

Her bag was checked at the station for incompletion. She was told that all her cotton was not accepted, and it was rejected.

They showed her the correct way in which she knew how to pick the cotton.

All the cotton was not in use. They threw the cotton away. She apologized and wasn't asked again to pick cotton. She was so happy because picking cotton was not her goal in life.

Heaven or hell cannot come into your life except if it is your will. We wrestle not against flesh and blood, against principalities, against powers, against the rulers of the darkness of this world, against spiritual wickedness in high places. We need the whole armor of God so that we may be able to withstand the evil day and have done all to stand.

Having your loins girt about with truth, and having on the breastplate, of righteousness. Above all, taking the shield of faith that we will be able to quench all the fiery darts of the wicked. Take the helmet of salvation and the sword of the spirit, which is the word of God.

Exie L. Smith was born in Montgomery, Alabama. Jim Crow laws were state and local, reinforcing racial segregation in the Southern United States. Because of segregation, she had a one-on-one conversation with God.

The Bible said in Romans 2:11, "For there is no respect of persons with God." She was anointed and appointed by God to serve others and praise God.

In Psalm 34:1, "I will bless the Lord at all times, his praises shall continually be in my mouth." She graduated from elementary school and George Washington Carver High School. She loved school and was an honor student. She graduated from Alabama State University.

TRANSITION

She made a transition to New York to fulfill her goals. She went to the board of education in New York, hoping to be hired as a teacher.

She was told by the members of the board of education that she needed fourteen credits to fulfill the requirements of New York.

She was not pleased with the decision of the members of the board of education. She was determined to make it. She wanted to be a teacher.

She enrolled at Hofstra University, determined to achieve her goals.

She graduated from Hofstra University with a master's degree of science in education in New Year, the day of October in the year of our Lord, in 1900.

She was hired by the board of education to teach school in the Dix Hill High School District in New York. She waited on the Lord for His blessing.

Trust in the Lord, with all thy heart. Lean not to your understanding but, in all thy ways, acknowledge Him, and He will direct our path.

"She made it."

Remedy of God

Jesus, my soul cries out hallelujah for saving me, "I made it." No earthly remedy can heal the widespread evil of the world.

I think faith has a remedy.

I think prayer has a remedy. I know God has a remedy.

I do not have to think about God. I know He has the remedy.

A long time ago, where Jesus led me, I will follow. I will go with Jesus all the way.

I will go with Jesus through the storm and the judgment.

Jesus can save and heal.

Hollywood Baptist Church

She joined Hollywood Baptist Church, pastored by Dr. Andy C. Lewter.

The spirit of praise and worship of the Lord was high. She knew how to bless the Lord, and it was at all times that the Lord's praise should continually be in her mouth.

Her soul shall make her boast in the Lord; the humble shall hear and be glad.

She sought the Lord, and He heard her and delivered her from all her fears.

She became a member of the Gospel Chorus and was one of the lead singers; she later became the president of the Gospel Chorus.

The Lord had his hands on her. She felt the anointing of the Holy Spirit.

Elder Exie L. Smith was called by God to preach the Gospel of Jesus Christ.

She was ordained by Pastor Dr. Andy C. Lewter to preach the Word of God.

Radio

Elder Exie L. Smith is on the Church Talk Radio, edi-fy-ng, empowering, enlightening, informing, and inspiring the people of God with the Word of God. The title is *Inspiration of the Good Shepherd.*

— Today is here; use it.
— Tomorrow is coming; prepare for it.
— Yesterday is gone; we profit from it.
— Remember, today is the first day of the rest of your life.

Schedule

Tuesday: 3:00–3:30 p.m.
Thursday: 3:00–3:30 p.m.
Saturday: 7:00–7:30 p.m.
Sunday: 6:00–6:30 p.m.

"She made it."

Sermons

Hold on to what you've got

Scripture: Job 28:12–28
Subject: Hold onto what you've got (philosophy of the wise)

1. Text: Job 28:12 says, "But where shall wisdom be found? And where is the place of understanding? And unto man he said, Behold, the fear of the Lord, that is wisdom; and to depart from evil is understanding." Subject: Hold Onto What You've Got
2. The alternate subject for this sermon is "The Philosophy of the Wise." If you have what it takes, you should be wise enough to hold onto what you've got. If you are otherwise, then you should be wise enough to get something worth holding onto. Though his name was not mentioned in the Old Testament, it foreshadows the One appearing in the New Testament; his name is Jesus. A wise

person is not only a hearer of the word but a doer of the word, one who has sustained faith in God. His faith is the sense or awareness of the soul by which he reaches God; have peace with God and have a piece of God. When you get this living relationship with God, *hold onto what you've got!*

3. If you cannot feel what you've got, you may lose it and not know it, so you ought to have such a hold on Christ and his hold on you until you have the realization that you've got something more precious than anything else, and you won't let go of it. So hold onto what you've got!

4. A lot of you know only one aspect of Job, so let me give you a summary of the Book of Job. The Book of Job is really a pastoral book, and you need to conceptualize it in that framework in order to understand it and appreciate its contents.

5. Job was a wealthy, blameless man, one who feared God and shunned evil. This hero of faith was picked out to be picked on, the one who was severely tested by the devil and experienced a crisis in life. He experienced a great loss: a loss of his earthly possessions, his economic wealth, and his social standing. His family was wiped out, his health was taken away, his friends turned against him, and he got sick and couldn't get well. On top of all that, his wife turned her back on him. Things went from bad to worse with Job, and his good name was threatened and tarnished. In the midst of his many personal crises—evil circumstances—

he struggled with the trust and confidence he had in God.

6. The interpretation of the great Jobian religious problems and those of contemporary man are basically the same, for all people experience problems common to human living. As in Job's case, learning how to cope with your problems is very essential to successful living. Job was steadfast amidst hard trials, and he held onto what he had, with the assurance that God, in His all-wise Providence, knew the reason why, and surely with God, things would eventually turn out all right!

7. If you are not able to properly deal with life through problem areas that sometimes bring on frustration and anxiety, it's liable to snap at you. You see, life is like a rubber band; it is flexible and able to adequately fit many circumstances, but if you keep on stretching it and put too much stress on it, it will snap on you. It is essential to get rid of some of that stress and tension to avoid going beyond the breaking point. Your faith in God makes a big difference in your ability to cope with life. I believe if you can see God in your circumstances and hold onto His unchanging hands, you will be able to cross over or go through your unpleasant circumstances. Never forget who you are and who you are! When you walk with God in the light of His word, you are walking on the highway of holiness, an heir of salvation, purchased of God, born of His Spirit, and washed in His blood. What we need to

remember is to pray! Have a little talk with Jesus; pray until you pray through; you may even reverse the charges because Jesus has paid the price.

8. Recently, we headed to New York, and we ran into a rainstorm so blinding that we could hardly see the road. We saw the emergency signals flashing on vehicles that had pulled off to the side of the road. My husband asked me if I thought we should do likewise and pull off to the side of the road. I said, "No, honey. I believe if we keep going, we will pass through the storm." You see, I remembered how once we were in a hailstorm and what we did. So I put on the windshield wiper to the fastest speed and put on the defroster to keep the windows clear, and we went on through the storm. After a while, just down the road a few miles from where others had stopped, the storm lifted, and there was no rain. Yes, we have our problems along life's busy way, but if we keep the faith and keep going, after a while, everything will turn out all right.

9. As long as we are in human form, we are going to experience problems common to human living. It is up to us to have sufficient faith to keep from going beyond the breaking point. A lot of emotional problems would be eliminated if you would come in for a checkup. A lot of marriages and families would last if you just came in for a checkup. God has given the Pastor the remedy for your needs. (The church would be better if the congregation would humble itself and come before the Lord in

prayer and holiness.) Counseling from the pastor and counseling from God will show you how to struggle through your problems. Not only that, a lot of you could keep a good job if you were able to put good counseling to work, hold your peace, and let God fight your battle! If you are already doing all this, hold onto what you've got!

10. Another thing we see within this book is interpersonal dynamics, something with a living force related directly to our mentality, our psychological or emotional, and our spiritual growth. This is the role of pastoral significance, whereby the pastor, as a counselor in the power of God, has been put here to reconcile the broken relationships throughout his congregation—the family of families—and show you that God (Christ) makes the difference. He may not have all the answers, but he knows the man who has them all. The Book of Job is recognized primarily for its valuable contributions to whatever answer there is to the universal question: Why man suffers? It is a serious investigation into whether one's loyalty to God is dependent upon him being favored by God.

11. Remember, when the devil was after Job, he had the nerve to tell God that the only reason Job serves you is because you have given him everything. Job was a very wealthy man with a good reputation, and he had a lot of friends. His great number of Campbells put him in a class all by himself, for they, in our time, equate to a nationwide trucking

system to carry supplies to needy areas. I believe we could safely say he had a monopoly on certain merchandise. But Job got sick and couldn't get well.

12. Job looked to himself; he looked to his wife, and he looked to his friends for the answer, but mundane minds didn't have the wisdom to supply the answer. He researched his theology, but theology failed him. He asked the great philosophers, but they could not supply the answer. He consulted the best doctors, and they couldn't prescribe the right medicine to cure his illness. Living is dangerous to your health. Tell me now, how did you feel when you had a similar experience, when, in the midst of prosperity, it seemed as though life's bottom fell out due to so many perplexing problems to which you didn't know the answer, and then you got sick and went to the hospital and the doctors said they couldn't help you, how did you feel? Job experienced the unexpected and learned how to deal with it.

13. Being a man in a bad fix, Job marked time with God. While searching himself, he rent his mantle, shaved his head, got down on his knees, and went in penitent prayer to God, remembering how he brought nothing into this world and that he would take nothing with him when he left; that the Lord gave, and the Lord hath taken away; blessed be the name of the Lord (Job 1:20–21). Out of Job's experience came unique awareness and knowledge

that God is the very source of wisdom, the One to whom he could turn for the answer!

14. God still has the answer to man's many perplexing problems! Earth has no sorrow that heaven cannot heal. When you trust in God and never doubt, you can hold your ground against great odds (James 1:12–18.) When the road gets rough and the going gets tough and the hills are hard to climb, if you would but claim His power, after a while, things will be all right, for all things work together for good to them that love the Lord (Romans 8:28.) The Jobian story (philosophy) is a path through which we may walk with sufficient strength to properly deal with life and maintain the joy of thy salvation! Out of Job's bad experience, over which he triumphed with the power of God, came a new awareness that his faith in God gave him something to hold onto! Out of his experience came the philosophy and advice that the fear of the Lord is wisdom, and to depart from evil is understanding (Job 28:28). Proverbs (4:7) says, "Wisdom is the principle thing: therefore get wisdom: and with all thy getting get understanding." James (1:5) says, "If any of you lack wisdom, let him ask of God, that giveth to all men liberally." The psalmist says, "The fear of the Lord is the beginning of wisdom: A good understanding have all they that do his commandments; his praise endureth forever" (Psalm 111:10). And Jesus says, "If you love me, keep my commandments" (John 14:23). "He

that gets this wisdom loves his own soul" (Proverbs 19:8). "He that gets this wisdom puts his destiny in God's hands" (Ecclesiastes 9:1). "If you are wise, you will come to know this Man of wisdom: God who established the world by wisdom" (Jeremiah 51:15) and made everything herein. "He that dwelleth in the secret place of the most high shall abide under the shadow of the Almighty" (Psalm 91:1).

15. Now let's pick up Job and close this thing out. You know, Job had three prominent friends, Eliphaz, Bildad, and Zophar, who heard about all this evil that had come upon Job. So they saw Job, and when they saw him in such a bad fix, they began to cry. And they sat down with Job seven days and seven nights (Job 2), no one saying a single word to Job, for they saw that his grief was great. After a while, I can hear them say, "Job, we are your friends, and we have come to pray with you." You know, when you first get sick and go to the hospital, your friends will visit you, but you just stay there a while, and then you will find out who your real friends are!

16. When Job didn't get well as quickly as they thought he should, they changed their minds about Job, turned their backs on him, and began to find fault in him. Job! You may not be everything you are coped up to be. According to the prevailing theology of retribution, you know, God blesses those who are really good, like you appear to be…but,

you see, we thought all the time…that you were a good man, especially when you showed your love by giving to the poor.

17. But due to your bad condition…God must be punishing you for something you did in the dark, and it has finally come to light. Well…all of you are wrong on your assumptions. I don't know what is happening to me now, but all my life, I've lived where God could use me, and I've walked uprightly in the pathway of duty; I have searched myself for any possible error but couldn't find and I even repented for any known or unknown sins of commission, omission, or disposition. I don't know what God is doing to me. I'm very sick now, and it looks as if I can't get well…but…I'm going to wait here on the Lord; the Lord giveth and the Lord taketh away; blessed be the name of the Lord. Though he slays me, yet will I trust in him: I'm going to wait. I'm going to wait on God until my change comes (Job 13:15).

18. I'm going to order my case before the Almighty; Lord, I'm searching for you! I know that my redeemer lives. I don't know how long it will take, but I'm going to wait on God; I'm going to hold onto what I've got. Tell me, after a while, God came to the scene in a whirlwind and talked with Job. "Job, I'm still with you," said the Lord. Job replied, "Lord, you've been with me in ages past. Through many dangers, toils, and snares you have brought me, you've been a shelter for me, and I

don't believe you brought me this far just to leave me. I'm waiting for you!" Job held onto his faith in God, and God rectified his situation and blessed him with twice as much as he had. Hold on! Hold on! Hold on! When your faith wavers, hope on anyhow! Hold on!

BE PREPARED

Scripture says, "Therefore be ye ready: for in such an hour as ye think not the Son of man cometh" (Matt 24:44).

INTRODUCTION

In 1909, Lord Baden Powell brought scouting to America. The motto of every good scout is to "be prepared." The motto does not support saying what kinds of things to be prepared for, but simply to be prepared for anything that comes.

Put simply, to prepare is to "get ready before the time comes."

Whether it is athletics, business, or secular education, the challenge is still the same, "get ready before the time comes."

There are three dimensions to the preparation of the Christian worker, which should all be fully developed. These are the preparation of the mind, attitude, and the heart.

The worker who is fully prepared has paid attention to the development of all three. While it is possible to get by without developing all three, our pledge should be to give our best to the master and settle for nothing less than excellence when it comes to the service of the Lord, whatever it costs, however much time it requires.

PREPARATION OF THE MIND

The preparation of the mind is the first of the three dimensions of Christian preparation.

God has given each of us great mental capabilities that can be used in his service. But like fertile but uncultivated fields, these abilities must cultivated before they can be of the best service for the Lord.

The national slogan of the United Negro College Fund also applies to church workers, "A mind is a terrible thing to waste."

God needs some workers who can think.

Christian workers find that thinking, as it relates to God's program, is best stimulated by the concentrated reading of God's word and the various methodologies utilized in its application, discussion, and participation in varied experiences.

Every Christian worker needs to provide certain quality time every week to stimulate their thoughts about the service of the Lord.

Thought stimulation requires time. It cannot be done in a hurry. If you are a church worker, we challenge you to be prepared by giving yourself time to think. Discuss. Read. Filter. Distill and apply.

Paul, writing to Timothy, encouraged the young man to think and study.

His encouragement is applicable today as well, "Study to show thyself approved, a workman that needeth not be ashamed but rightly diving the works of truth."

His words are encouraging as he encourages us by saying that whatever things are pure, just, good, lovely, think on these.

PREPARATION OF THE ATTITUDE

The second dimension of preparation is that of attitude. It is possible to be a thinker but fail in our work because of an unprepared attitude.

Attitude is based upon faith in God and willingness to obey his will, whatever the cost.

Many of the Lord's finest servants began with an attitude problem but were prepared for service by the hand of God.

Jonah had an attitude problem. He refused to serve because he didn't want good things to happen to his enemies.

Jonah had an attitude problem, but the Lord prepared him for service by working on his attitude.

The Lord prepared a fish to retrieve him from the mouth of death.

He prepared a gourd to protect him from the scorching rays of the sun.

And when he became complacent and comfortable, he prepared a worm to chew down the gourd.

The Lord can change attitudes. Thus, prepared to serve, Jonah went out and preached an uncompromising Gospel to the people of Nineveh and saved a whole nation.

Jeremiah had an attitude problem at the beginning of his service. He said, "Lord, I am just a young person. I don't want to deal with these people. They are set in their ways. They will work against me in every way and assassinate my character."

Jeremiah had a pessimistic and defeatist attitude. He was whipped before he began. But the Lord went to work on his attitude.

I hear the Lord saying, "Don't say that I am a child, but while you were still in your mother's womb, I put my hands on you and gave you a job to do. Be not afraid of their frowning faces and the biting remarks. Go forward in my name."

Peter had an attitude problem. He didn't want the Gospel message to go around the world, but the Lord worked on his attitude.

Saul had an attitude problem, but Lord stopped him one day on the Damascus road and worked on his attitude.

Every Christian worker should be conditioned to the attitude that we are in service for God and not for the praise of man.

If the crowds don't receive your service with accolades of praise, serve on anyhow.

If you find yourself working and it seems like you are all by yourself, serve on anyhow.

Remember what Dr. Watts said, "A charge to keep I have, a God to glorify, an ever-dying soul to save and fit it for the sky."

Keep on serving because one of these days, the Lord is coming, and he'll declare, "Servant, servant, well done."

PREPARATION OF THE HEART

It is good to have a prepared mind. It is also good to have a prepared attitude of commitment, but none of these are any good unless you have a prepared heart.

Jesus made the case one day when he spoke to the rich young ruler.

The young ruler said he had prepared his mind through a diligent study of the law. He said he had prepared his attitude through an unwavering attitude of obedience to the laws of God. He felt like his developed mind and attitude of commitment made him ready to enter the kingdom.

But Jesus said, "There is one thing thou lackest: sell all you have, take up your cross, and follow me."

There are many who study the word diligently and work aggressively, but they are still trying to hold on to the world and work in the kingdom at the same time.

Jesus made the point clear to Nicodemus, "You must be born again."

Every child of God knows that you can't serve effectively until you have had a meeting with the Lord.

Isaiah said, "Lord, I'm not worthy to serve. My mouth is filled with foul words, and my mind is filled with evil thoughts."

God prepared him to serve by sending an angel to touch his lips with hot coal and urge away his iniquities.

God will prepare our hearts if we ask him to give us clean hearts and lives.

After Isaiah had a meeting with the Lord, he declared for the world to hear, "In the year King Uzziah Died, I met the Lord."

"If the Lord needs somebody, here am I send me / If the Lord needs somebody, though the winds may blow, I'll go! / If the Lord needs somebody, though the storms may rise, I'll go!"

For one of these mornings, he's coming back again, for I heard him say, "I go prepare a place for you that where I am, ye may be also."

One of these mornings, I'm going home.

One of these mornings, I'm going to say, "Goodbye time, hello eternity."

I've got to be ready when Jesus comes. Be ready!

Be prepared!

After a while, it'll all be over!

OPPOSITE TO THE DEVIL

We are confronted daily with the tactics, the tricks, and the devices of the devil. Satan is not in hell now. He is not locked up in the bottomless pit (as he will be someday). He is the "god of his age," walking up and down, going to and fro, seeking to drag men and women away from Christ, trying to see who he can derail. He is doing his level best to drag each one of us down to defeat and destruction. It seems that Satan is working overtime these days because he knows that his time is limited. He is away, but shortly, he will be cast into the lake of fire, where he will be tormented day and night forever and ever. See Revelation 20:10. But until that time, how can we overcome his onslaughts?

> Submit yourselves to God. Resist the devil, and he will flee from you. (James 4:7)

> Greater is he that is in you than he that is in the world. (I John 4:4)

In order to overcome the devices of the devil, we must surrender our lives to God and receive Jesus into our hearts by faith.

When a person takes these steps, he becomes a new creative with new desires and with new power to overcome temptation.

All of us find that living the Christian life involves ongoing warfare. We are to put on the whole armor of God, that ye may be able to stand against the wiles of the devil.

We wrestle not against flesh and blood but against principalities, against the rustlers of the darkness of this world, against spiritual wickedness. In high places, take unto you the whole armor of God, that ye may be able to withstand in the evil day, having done all to stand. Stand having your loins girt about with truth and having on the breastplate of righteousness. Have your feet shod with the preparation of the gospel of peace, above all taking the shield of faith, that we will be able to quench all the fiery darts of the wicked. Take the helmet of salvation and the sword of the Spirit, which is the Word of God.

Praying always with all prayer and supplication in the Spirit, watching with all perseverance and supplication for all saints, the only hope of this world is for us to return to Christ Jesus.

Every child of God is encouraged to "seek ye first the kingdom of heaven and its righteousness and all the other things will be added." Every good deed is added to your treasure in heaven. Every kind word added a star to your crown. With every gift of time and finance, God will add another star to your crown. Every prayer prayed for the lost and weary, another star God will add to your crown. "I am sending up my timber every day. I'm laying up the treasure in heaven's stable land." There are many people today who have not been convinced of the power of prayer. Every child of God is reminded to pray without ceasing. Regardless of what the skeptics say, prayer changes things. Prayer can move incredible mountains. Prayer can lift us from the valley of despairs. Prayer can resolve difficulties and maintain peace. Prayer can change the direction of wayward lives to love one another. Prayer is the key to the kingdom; faith unlocks the door. Sometimes in life, it seems like the day will break. Sometimes in life, it gets so dark. Sometimes in life, it seems like joy has gone astray, and all hopes have faded away. Sometimes in life, the problems of life make many of us believe it's too late. Sometimes, it makes us feel the hour has passed. Sometimes in life, the problems of life make the heart throb and ache.

But our God is an omnipotent, omniscient, and omnipresent God. Nothing is impossible with God. In the Christian life, we battle against powerful evil forces headed by Satan. To withstand his attacks, we must depend on God's strength and use every piece of armor that is provided. All believers are special objects of Satan's attacks because they are no longer on Satan's side. We need supernatural power to defeat Satan. God has provided that power through the Holy Spirit, who lives within us and by the provision of armor that surrounds us. What a friend we have in Jesus, all our sins and griefs to bear! What a privilege to carry everything to God in prayer. Oh, what peace we often forfeit;

oh, what needless pain we bear, all because we do not carry everything to God in prayer. Take it to Jesus.

Have we trials and temptations? Is there trouble anywhere? We should never be discouraged; take it to the Lord in prayer. Can we find a friend so faithful who will share all our sorrow? Jesus knows our every weakness; take it to the Lord in prayer.

It may be troubles. It may be misfortunes; it may be misunderstanding. It may be heartache, it may be disappointment, it may be suffering, it may be crying, it may be weeping. Take it to the Lord in prayer.

He may not come when you want him, but He is always on time. Take it to the Lord in prayer. Take it to the Lord.

Thou art my God, the strength of my salvation. God has covered my head on the day of battle. Teach me, Lord, to do Thy will, for Thou art my God; my Spirit is good. Lead me into the land of uprightness. Quicken me, O Lord, for Thy namesake; for the righteousness's sake, bring my soul out of trouble. For the Lord taketh pleasure in his people; He will beautify the meek with salvation. Let the saints be joyful in glory; let everything that hath breath praise the Lord, praise the Lord.

The Surrendered Life

Scripture: Romans 6:13
Introduction:

When we become Christian, God requires that we surrender our life. God's will is that sinful attitudes and actions should be put to death in the Christian's life, his nature and character renewed after the image of God in Christ, and his obedience to God increased so that he lives to please God.

I. A Christian's eyes should be surrendered
    A. Surrendered eyes will study the Bible (Psalm 1:2)
    B. Surrendered eyes will look to Jesus (Hebrews 12:2)
    C. Surrendered eyes will look for the lost (John 4:35)

II. A Christian's ears should be surrendered.
    A. Surrendered ears are deaf to gossip (I Timothy 4:7; 6:20)

B. Surrendered ears are opened to Jesus's word (Luke 10:39)
   C. Surrendered ears are obedient to God's message (Acts 8:26, 27)

III. A Christian's tongue should be surrendered
   A. A surrendered tongue is bridled (James 1:26)
   B. A surrendered tongue is prayerful (I Timothy 2:1–4)
   C. A surrendered tongue will tell about Jesus (Mark 5:19, 20)

IV. A Christian's hands should be surrendered
   A. Surrendered hands do not steal (Ephesians 4:28)
   B. Surrendered hands will help those in need (Hebrews 12:12)
   C. Surrendered hands will make right the wrong (Acts 16:33)

V. A Christian's feet should be surrendered
   A. Surrendered feet are upon a rock (Psalm 40:2)
   B. Surrendered feet are shod with the gospel (Ephesians 6:15)
   C. Surrendered feet will bruise Satan (Romans 16:20)

VI. A Christian's Heart Should Be Surrendered
   A. Surrendered heart is clean (Psalm 51:10)

B. Surrendered heart is Christ indwelled (Ephesians 3:17)
   C. Surrendered heart will do God's will sage (Ephesians 6:6)

VII. A Christian's whole body should be surrendered
   A. Surrendered body is God's workmanship (Ephesians 2:10)
   B. A surrendered body is a sacrifice to God (Romans 12:1)
   C. A surrendered body is the temple of the Holy Ghost (1 Corinthians 6:19)

There Is Power in Tears

Jeremiah 9:1

> "Oh, that my head were waters, and mine eyes a fountain of tears, that I might weep day and night for the slain of the daughter of my people!" Is. 22:4:–10:19

Jeremiah was born a priest and ordained by God to be a prophet. Jeremiah told God he wasn't mature or worthy of the prophetic title because he was a child. God told Jeremiah, "Say not thy art a child, for thou shall go to all I send thee. And whatsoever I command thee, thou shall speak." Jeremiah labored for some forty years.

Jeremiah gave more details of his life than any other Old Testament prophet. His ministry was intensely sad, and his song was in the minor key. It was melancholy that made his head water and his eyes a fountain of tears. Because the truth he had to proclaim was unwelcome and brought him enemies, he carried out his task without fear of favor (ver. 1) (theme). In these days of national apostasy and international strife, the preacher could not do better than to live near the word of God, with true religion in his heart and life in the church and nation.

Jeremiah lived a life of loneliness. inconspicuous, losing himself among strangers who cared not for him. Jeremiah did not seek the luxury of grief, or did he seek to evade the duties of a preacher's life. He did not seek to evade the impending dangers he had announced, not to intermit his spiritual activities.

Jeremiah is not seeking solitude or spiritual detachment in the midst of busy thronging transgressors. He wanted to get away from it all, to weep for the slain daughters of his people. He wanted to find him a crying place. He wanted to study the problem. He wanted to recover his mental and spiritual claim. He wanted to recruit his spiritual energies for a new and more successful effort. So it is in our lives today. There are times when we want to get away from it all.

Many times, we have to take a vacation from the hustle and bustle. Sometimes, we need to be influenced by God's word. Because we oftentimes live too close to our problems to see them. Just want to get away from it all (ver. 1–2).

Our society today is of that of Jeremiah. Everywhere, there is moral duplicity of the people. Yet they refuse to recognize how they bring their evil upon themselves. Our nation is filled with indignation. Every brother is a Jacob, intending to destroy his brother. May we catalog several of the sins that make us cry. Tongue slandering, deceitfulness, lying, and double-dealing. All of this must be thrown back upon the fact. The vast majority of our society does not know God. When you cannot save people after preaching, teaching, and praying, there is only one other alternative, and that is to weep for them (ver. 1) (theme).

It is unusual and a strange, sad sight to see a strong man in tears. But here is Jeremiah, who appears utterly broken down. His tears remind us of those of our Lord and Paul. Paul said to the Corinthian church (2 Corinthians 2:4) that tears were a relief to the overburdened heart, like the cry of a sufferer in sore pain. Seemingly, just the cry will relieve some of the miseries or hasten God's mercy to relieve it all. Many people are glad when they behold their fellow man enduring some crushing sorrow. And pouring forth their grief in tears. But Jeremiah felt tears to be a relief. When sorrows lie too deep for tears, then sorrows become greater than we can bear.

Tears are admonitory, which means they express a warning of oversights, faults, or friendliness. Tears bear a very powerful testimony. And we all will do well to give heed to them because they bear witness. Anytime you see a person crying, that says something to us.

We wonder why? What happened? Or who did it? Tears make us wonder (ver. 1) (theme), but we see God's servants, such as Jeremiah, Paul, and others, laboring with all energy of the soul, with infinite self-sacrifice, exposed to every form of ill with many tears. We are constrained to inquire about the motive of such life.

> What shall we then say to these things? If God be for us, who can be against us?

He that spared not his own Son, but delivered him up for us all, how shall he not with him also freely give us all things?

Who shall lay any thing to the charge of God's elect? It is God that justifieth.

Who is he that condemneth? It is Christ that died, yea rather, that is risen again, who is even at the right hand of God, who also maketh intercession for us.

Who shall separate us from the love of Christ? *shall* tribulation, or distress, or persecution, or famine, or naked-ness, or peril, or sword?

As it is written, For thy sake we are killed all the day long; we are accounted as sheep for the slaughter.

Nay, in all these things we are more than conquerors through him that loved us.

For I am persuaded, that neither death, nor life, nor angels, nor principalities, nor powers, nor things present, nor things to come.

I MADE IT

> Nor height, nor depth, nor any other creature, shall be able to separate us from the love of God, which is in Christ Jesus our Lord. (Romans 8:31–39)

Anyone who does not believe there is power in tears is an unconscious agent with a bewildered and disordered brain that will not stand investigation (theme). Tears are no falsehood. They will live in every eye and acquire power over every mind. No sympathetic heart can look at all the wickedness in the land. All of the sin around us and all of the suffering in our eyes, without shedding a tear sometimes. If you are a believer in God, pray honestly. The power of God, which overshadows Him, will bring tears from the eyes. One cannot begin to think of His blessings or remember the miracle that God has wrought in Him without shedding some tears.

When one has been won to Christ and turned from their wicked ways, those who know the compassion of God for His own soul will, in proportion, feel compassion for the soul of others (ver.

C) 1) (theme). Jeremiah would have been unworthy of his call and his vision as a prophet if he had fallen short of the exclamation of protest and outcry. Crying was no put-on with Jeremiah. Tears were the index of his heart. Jeremiah was not weeping over some spoiled gratification of self. He rather wept when he saw his people going heedlessly into perdition. He wept because of their eternal damnation into hell. Jeremiah wept when he looked deep into the confusion of his time. Yet he did not see as deep as

Jesus. Those tears that Jesus dropped amid the bereaving agonies of Bethany had in them more of a pure and profound pity over men than all the tears of our Christian nation and repenting sinners put together (theme).

Man can never imagine how far Jesus was discerning when He wept over the holy city. Jesus wept because He knew how far man had fallen from his Creator. Plus, He knew how high fallen men could be raised. He knew what a man misses when he does not repent and believe in Him. He could see the possibilities of remorse, shame, and self-condemnation opening up in eternity to the negligent and impenitent people. Those who choose to see the wind and forget must reap the whirlwind (ver. 1) (theme).

David cried over the sins of his son Absalon, just as Jeremiah cried over his people. And Jesus wept for Jerusalem when Jesus's compassionate heart was grievous; tears of sorrow filled the cup that is treasured in Him. He wept because He loved the world. Which His father gave Him. He that goeth forth weepeth, bearing precious seeds, shall come again rejoicing. They that sow in tears reap in joy (theme). Weeping sometimes endures all through the night, but joy cometh in the morning (theme). Jesus said, "Blessed are they that hunger now, for they shall be filled. Blessed are they that weep now, for they shall laugh." (theme)

Touching God through Prayer

Scripture: II Chronicles 14:9–12
Introduction:

"To be effective, a prayer must go through the forces of spiritual darkness and touch God. In order to touch God and receive an answer, man must be conditioned in his own heart" (I John 3:21). Let us look at Asa's prayer that we might receive some guidelines.

1. He was praying for the welfare of others.
2. He was praying in a crisis of emergency.
3. God answered his prayer.

I. The characteristics of his prayer
    A. He prayed in earnest, "Asa cried…"
        1. He felt the immediate need.
        2. He recognized his personal responsibility in relation to people.
        3. He knew he must lead the way.

B. In his prayer, he was brief and to the point.
   1. He didn't pray around the world.
   2. He needed divine help immediately.
   3. He had faith that God would hear his prayer and answer.
   4. Because he was in good standing with God—and prayed up to date. Asa could pray in this manner.

C. His prayer was personal.
   1. Asa cried to "his God."
   2. Asa could recognize a relationship with God.
   3. He believed God understood, sympathized, and would help.

D. Asa's praying was specific and definite.
   1. Prayer should be specific and definite. Asa told the Lord who was in need, "Help us."
   2. He knew that their only source of deliverance was God (Deuteronomy 33:29)
      a. He acknowledges their dependence on God.
      "We rest on thee" (Numbers 14:8).
      b. He acknowledges the importance of faith.
   3. He trusted in the divine promise (2 Kings 18:5)

4. The certainty of obedience
   a. Sometimes, it takes more courage to wait on God than to rush on into battle (Hebrews 4:16, 13:6).
   b. He appealed to the promises of God
   c. He recognized the great character of God.

1 Chronicles 29:12

II. Asa's prayer was answered (verses 12–15)
   A. God delivered them from the enemy.
   B. They achieved a great victory (Genesis 14–15, Exodus 14:30).

III. Any Christian can be effective in prayer
   A. God is no respecter of persons
   B. He is within reach of all
   C. He will hear the cry of all (Psalm 34:1–10).

Conclusion

In any and every circumstance in life, we have the blessed assurance that we can have God's help. Are you effective in your prayer life? Can you touch God?

EXCEPT A MAN BE BORN AGAIN

Scripture: "Jesus answered and said unto him, Verily, verily, I say unto thee, Except a man be born again, he cannot see the kingdom of God" (John 3:3).

INTRODUCTION

When Former President Jimmy Carter took office in 1976, he became one of the first presidents to openly express that he was a born-again Christian.

The nation was generally accustomed to the term "born again" because it had been applied loosely to describe a variety of changes of direction that were affecting the country. Racists, who once spoke against integration, had begun to court a growing Black voting electorate. The nation tagged this reformation by men such as Alabama's George Wallace as being "born again."

Being born is not a tactic or a political maneuver shrewdly employed to gain an advantage. It is not a tongue-in-cheek phrase used to describe any switch in position.

To be born again is to have a new life in Christ.

To be born again is to have a new attitude in Christ.

To be born again is to have a new direction and purpose in Christ.

President Carter ignored his critics and continued to own his new life in Christ without shame and embarrassment.

Today, every Christian should wear our born-again status as a badge of honor.

Every day, we should commit ourselves to witnessing and serving his cause, no matter what the world might say, because one day, he's coming to call the born again to live again with him in paradise.

–I–
The Secret Christians

Our text first considers Nicodemus, one of the three richest men in Jerusalem and a member of the Sanhedrin council. He was a man of considerable influence among the Jews, immense popularity and well connected and respected.

With respect to Jesus, we see Nicodemus in three places in the book of John. We see him meeting Jesus in John 3:2, leaning toward supporting Jesus at his trial in 7:50–51, and coming to wrap the body of Jesus in 19:39.

In each instance, Nicodemus was careful to hide his support of Jesus. Verse 19:38 says specifically that he came "secretly" to avoid negative feedback from the community.

Nicodemus could easily be described as a secret Christian! He was attracted to the Gospel message, the Savior himself, and desired to enter the kingdom of heaven, but he feared the wrath of his neighbors. He did many good things to help the cause, but he never openly confessed Christ himself.

Brothers and sisters, there are a great number of people in the church who are active participants in worldly things. But there are also a larger number of people in the world who secretly desire to be in the church.

They suffer from the Nicodemus syndrome. They want to secretly serve the Lord without their friends knowing it.

They listen to music about Christ! They read literature about Christ! They listen to sermons on the radio and television about Christ! They even support religious projects with their finances, but they won't come forward to own Christ as their personal savior!

There may be two reasons for their reluctance. First, they overestimate the importance of their friends and neighbors.

Many worry about what their friends and neighbors will say.

We who have laboriously worked to develop a reputation among our friends as the foxiest, cutest, finest, most exciting, enticing, vivacious worry about what people will say if they say, "She used to be hot to trot, but now she's a Christian."

We who have expended all of our resources to impress our friends that we are the handsomest, baddest, coolest, toughest, the save, debonair, the chastity killers and the women killers worry about what our friends will say if they say, "He used to be cool, but now he's a Christian."

We say to you today that the Christian life does not make you any less handsome or debonair, foxy or cute, but it does make you feel a whole lot better on the inside.

To those who want to be Christians but are ashamed to let their friends know, we remind them of Jesus's words in Luke 9:26, "Whosoever shall be ashamed of me and my words, of him shall the Son of man be ashamed when he shall come into his glory."

To those who worry about what their friends will say, we would like to introduce you to a friend that "sticketh closer than a brother."

No wonder two songwriters declared, "I have found a friend, who is all the world to me, his love is ever true," and "What a friend we have in Jesus."

Secondly, there are some secret Christians who won't come to Christ because they underestimate the power of the Lord!

They feel that if they come out of the world and openly confess Christ and their newfound faith does not hold, they will wind up back in the world.

They feel that the power of the Holy Spirit alone is not sufficient to keep them from drifting back into the world and becoming a laughingstock of their neighborhood.

But I hear Paul talking to the Lord on three separate occasions, asking to get relief from a thorn in his side and looking for alibis to be excused from the service, and God's response in 2 Corinthians 12:9 was "My grace is sufficient for thee."

Those who abandon their secret life and come forward for the Lord will find that He will hold them in the hollow of His hand.

He will give you a new song. Instead of singing "I've got the down home blues," you'll sing "Jesus, Jesus, Jesus, sweetest name I know, fills my every longing, keeps me singing as I go!"

–II–
You Must Be Born Again!

Finally, brothers and sisters, Jesus told Nicodemus, "Except a man be born again, he can't enter into the kingdom of heaven."

That word "except" is used in at least six other places talking about conversion.

In Luke 13:3, "Except ye repent, ye shall perish likewise."

In Matthew 18:3, "Except ye be converted and become as little children, ye shall not enter the kingdom of heaven."

In John 3:5, "Except a man be born of the water and of the spirit, he cannot enter into the kingdom of heaven."

In John 6:53, "Except ye eat the flesh of the Son of man, and drink his blood ye have no life in you."

In John 15:4, "Except ye abide in me, you cannot be saved."

But here, I hear Jesus saying, "Except a man be born again, he cannot enter into the kingdom of God."

You can get to heaven without seeing Niagara Falls and walking through the grand canyon, but you can't get to heaven without being born again!

You can get to heaven:

- owning a Rolls Royce or a ten-carat diamond ring
- having an overflowing bank account or a stylish wardrobe
- without a high school diploma or a PhD
- without wearing a soft mink coat or touching the liberty bell
- without listening to the music of Beethoven or marching in a parade
- writing a best-selling book or being a star on Broadway

But you can't get to heaven without being born again!

To be born again is not reformation, for that's the same creature in a new suit.

To be born again is not church membership, for that's the same man with his name on a church roll!

To be born again, you must abandon purposes and activities that take you away from God!

To be born again, you reach out to God in the name of Jesus!

To be born again, you must tear down the old house and build up a new house.

I heard a songwriter say, "I moved from my old house, I moved from my old friends, and my old way of life. Thank God I've got a brand-new life."

Standing on the Rock

(Matthew 7:24–27)

Jesus turns from the judgment of the teaching in the parable of the tree and the fruit to the judgment of the hearers in the parable that is now before us (ver. 24) (theme). A rock is not a bed of simple minerals. A rock is a sedimentary stratum overlying mass of plutonic minerals bound together in the form of crystal cement, materially speaking. But in the spiritual realm, Christ himself is the (Rock), for the psalmist says, "The Lord is my rock, and my fortress, and my deliverer; My God, my strength, in whom I will trust; My buckler, and the horn of my salvation, and my high tower" (Psalm 18:2). The psalmist further says, "He is my rock and my salvation. He is my defense. I shall not be moved" (Psalm 62:6). The psalmist says, "Thy art my Father, My God and the Rock of my Salvation" (Psalm 61:2). He further said when he had gotten lost from God Lead me to the rock that is higher than I; What David is actually saying, lead me to God where I can find safety and peace. All who believe in the fullness of Christ are in accord with the subject. (Theme)

All other grounds are sinking sand. It does not matter how solid the surface may appear to be. There is no more security of safety than to place all confidence and trust in God. Paul also tells us in 1 Corinthians 10:1–4, "That Rock is Christ." He is the source and author of all blessings in every period of history and in all circumstances of humanity. The Rock died for all mankind in every age. His presence never moves, and his grace never fails. (Stand on the rock) As Jesus elaborates on the parable in the sermon on the mountain. The parable said that He Himself was the Rock. Jesus drew this parable because it was particularly vivid in His own country.

Nazareth is built in a cleft of hills; some of its houses are purchased on jotting rocks. A similar character of foundations was found in the neighborhood of Gennesaret, where Jesus is now teaching. History is also illustrated in the plans of Sharon. The clay is so inferior that jars can make houses worthless. Jesus is saying to us that storms come at an unexpected time. Therefore, he is admonishing us to prepare for the forceable storms, for we know in life that the sun will not always shine or will calm and dry weather last forever (theme).

In this parable, Jesus is also preparing us for the unexpected, tempestuous wind. And the beating of the rain. (Ver. 24) Any house that stands against inclement weather must be well substantiated. Therefore, the parabolic words of Jesus illustrate two types of houses. The house, which is built on the rock, demonstrates a moral attitude and religious principles in life, which means that it is built on the rock. (Ver. 24–25) The house that is built on the sand gives us a paradoxical view of self that is contradictory. Because he who built his house on sand opposed to common sense. (Theme)

Look how Jesus emphasizes the loss at the expense of foolishness. (Ver. 26–27) This house is not standing on the rock. Living is building. Every day that we live in this life, we are building on our house. It takes a lifetime and all of life's works to put together our habitation in which we will have to dwell. Some people build so feebly by setting up weak structures or mere huts and shanties. Some work with ambitious designs; some make themselves spacious mansions and some gorgeous places, and some make massive castles. But whatever a man builds here, that he must dwell in, in the hereafter. We cannot get away from the results of our life's work, whether it is a shelter to protect the soul or a ruin for the lost soul.

If this is what we build, this must we dwell in. I would like to encourage you to build for Jesus. (You understand) The security of THE building is determined by the solidity or solidness of the foundation. If the foundation is rotten, the greater the building, the more insecure it will be. And the greater will be the fall there of when it comes down. So I encourage you, In spite of what may come or who may go, build on Jesus (Matthew 5:18). (Theme)

It is vain and foolish for a man to bestow his care on towers and pinnacles while the foundation is giving away.

All efforts are spent merely on ornamentation or decorative waste. In practical life, this is the last thing. Many people consider that decoration is the first thing that will wear out on us. For as soon as we are looked over and speculated, we are forgotten. People nowadays would rather build on a name for fame than build on a real-life for Christ. They would rather order setups on the rock than stand on the true Rock, which is Christ. People want good fruit, but they don't want to graft them from the right stock. They want to be rewarded with eternal life in the judgment. Yet while they lived, their goal was never to go through the straight gate. If you want eternal life for the soul, you have to reach for the right goal. Stand on the right Rock, unwavering, undoubting in faith. (Ver. 24)

The question is, what are you building on? Troubles and trials? Misfortunes and persecutions are the test of whether we are building on sand or rock. What are you building on? You may say from the lips that you are building on faith. This is good to say in words. But it is better to prove it in reality. Faith works in persecution, troubles, trials, and tribulations. In all of these, we must have perseverance and obedience.

The only living faith in Christ proves its existence by bringing forth fruit to God in active service. (Theme)

Story

One man built his house on the sand, and the other man built his house on the rock. Both started at the same time. Both of them had planned to retire when they finished with their houses. Both of them had promised their families all of the comforts that this world had to offer.

So the man who built on the rock made but little progress. And every day at noontime, his wife would bring his lunch to him. The man who had no foundation house was going up rapidly. But the one on the foundation was still digging trenches. His wife decided that she would question her husband, who was still building on the foundation. She said, "That man over there has almost got his house completed. Why is it that it's taking you so long? The winter will set in, and we won't be moved."

The husband said, "The reason that it is taking so long is that when the storm comes, the house will stand."

So after many months, the man who built on the foundation also finished it. Then the winter came. The house that was built on sand, when it began to rain, the water washed all of the sand from around the house, and the rain beat upon it, and the wind did blow. The house fell. And great was its fall. But the house on the foundation withered the storm because it was built upon a rock. (Theme)

There are three persons involved in building a house. Firstly, the architect is the one who creates or designs the house. Secondly, the contractor is the one who erects the house. And thirdly, the state inspector, the one who approves the house. So it is with the Godhead of divinity. There are three who have prominently shared the soul. God the Father has a creative share of the soul because He is the creator. God the Son has a redemptive share in the soul because He paid the price for our sins with His redemptive blood. God the Holy Ghost proves and keeps the soul. The Rock is Jesus. When the storms of life rise, He shelters me with a love of aspiration. He shelters me with love and light to higher spiritual responsibilities.

Let the wind blow. Let troubles flood the life. Let afflictions afflict life. The Lord promised if I stay on the Rock, He will keep me safe. I am standing on the Rock of Salvation, which is able to sustain me. He is able. He is able to carry you through.

Waiting on God

> But they that wait upon the Lord shall renew
> their strength; they shall mount up with wings
> as eagles; they shall run, and not be weary;
> and they shall walk, and not faint.
>
> —Isaiah 40:31

Waiting upon God is not a lazy man's way out of difficulties. It is not good and healthy for the soul or body, which has become laden with burdens because of sin. Waiting upon God is a Christian's grace. It is developed through a heart's faith and a soul's hope. True and Christian waiting upon God means that a person has exhausted all of his resources to do so. He has used every effort to bring to pass the right desire of his heart. Then he leaves the victory, honor, glory, and majesty to God. He waits on God to fill the need, answer the prayer, cure the sick, remove sin, and let righteousness reign.

Many who live this morning are without knowledge of God's goodness and His grace. They feel that this is just another day in which they live because they have earned it.

I am glad that I know that I earned it, not this day. No man lives because he deserves it. We live, but God Almighty has suspended nature, dropped mercy in the path of death, placed His foot of longevity on many careening automobiles, and wrote over many doorposts "another chance" with the blood of the Lamb.

We live, but God the Reigning King with the scepter of grace has made every form of nature a bodyguard. Winds that would have destroyed our bodies only chilled and comforted us; cold weather that would have carried our souls where no one has returned to tell the story has only taken away the germs that wanted just another day to attack us.

One is never forsaken to wait on God. It is He who, out of the darkness and most confused day, walks up and down every street, visits every home, and examines every soul. From this examination, He finds somebody waiting. He yet sends His Spirit to some soul to comfort His people. His voice is still heard, and he cries loudly until the appointed time. Somebody may become a follower of God. For that reason, He continually tells a messenger to cry, comfort, prepare the way of the Lord, and make straight in the desert a highway for God. Root up and cover—fill the valleys of dry bones and degradation. Tear down the mountains and hills of sin in high places, and the glory of the Lord shall be revealed, and all flesh shall see it together. Men will sing for the royal crown and tell Him who made us to ride and reign on.

I MADE IT

Waiting on God implies

I. A special recognition of God

It means that we have a sense of our own weakness. In this attitude, we'll know that we are unable to get on without Him. We seek His divine aid and his lamblike care and wait and recognize His word. His word will stand forever:
David says that it is hidden in his heart.

1. Trust in the Lord with all thine heart.
2. Rest in the Lord, and wait patiently for Him.
3. Wait for the Lord, be of good cheer, and he shall strengthen thy heart.
4. Vengeance is mine—I will repay.
5. Trust in the Lord and do good so shall thou inherit the land.

We must give recognition to the God of our Salvation. He will come; His reward is with Him; His work is before Him. She shall feed His flock like a shepherd.

We must recognize the strength of our God. We cannot become doubtful or afraid.

Wait on Him.

II. An earnest desire

We cannot play waiting on God. Sin is raging, and doubt is all about us. The valley of the shadow of death is dense. The world is foggy. Through all that darkens the soul and blinds the eye until His voice is ____. His presence is felt, His power is seen, and His way is made known. Says one of old, "Thy soul waiteth for the Lord more than they that watch for the morning."

He strengthens the feeble knee;
Rejoices the sorrowful heart;
Gives life to the fainting body;
And revives tho wavering life.

That waiting for God,

III. Means

1. Service
2. Keeping near

He giveth power to the faint and to them that have no might.

The youth shall faint and be weary, and young men shall utterly fall.

Are you waiting on Him who shall one day call you from labor to reward? If not, decide today to put your trust in one who is able to keep you from falling into the hands of wicked men of this world.

Trust in God with all thine heart, and he shall give you every need.

No Easy Road to Walk

Scripture: "That this may be a sign among you, that when your children ask their fathers in time to come saying, What mean ye by these stones? Then ye shall answer them, that the waters of the Jordan were cut off before the ark of the covenant of the Lord; when it passed over Jordan, the waters of Jordan were cut off and these stones shall be for a memorial unto the children of Israel for ever" (Joshua 4:6–7).

INTRODUCTION

The road to freedom has not been an easy one to travel. It has carried us through a meandering path that has wound through tragedy and triumph.

We have lived through the tragedy of slavery and have felt its sting on our families for eighteen generations. We stumbled along the way and lost considerable ground as we slid down the rocky hillsides of obstacles and roadblocks.

Many giants have fallen as they led us to this day. The roadside is bespeckled with reminders of their personal sacrifices that have helped us reach this point.

Freedom's road has been tedious and, at times, treacherous, swallowing the will of thousands who started out but gave up along the way.

But while the road was filled with tragedies and casualties, it was also filled with triumphs and victories.

We have seen doors, once closed in our faces, opened. The children of slaves now consider themselves equal to the children of slave masters.

We have won the right to be free, vote, and receive justice under the law.

We have won many victories, but they have not come easy.

How is it that a people enslaved for 250 years in chains and another 125 years in mental manacles can look back and see anything for which to be thankful?

We are thankful because we know that without God on our side, our plight would never have changed.

The Black man's hope and dependence on the Lord sustained him as he walked this lonely road.

Every now and then, we stop and take a peek at the ground we have covered and give thanks to God for the strength he gave us to make every step of the way.

This has not been an easy journey for us, but without God, it would have been no journey at all.

-I-

Our text first considers Israel as they make their way into the promised land. Moses, the great lawgiver, has died, and Joshua is leading the people. They have crossed the

I MADE IT

River Jordan, and now on the other side, they set up history markers to mark the place where the Lord led them through to the land of their dreams.

Joshua commanded the Israelites to set up twelve stones in the middle of the river and twelve stones on the riverside. The twelve huge stones set atop each other in the riverbed could be seen from the bank, and those on the shore would serve as reminders of what God had done for them.

When generations to come would see the strange arrangements of stones and ask, "What mean these stones?" they would be given an opportunity to tell the story of the long journey home.

For Israel, the journey included four hundred years of slavery, a period of wandering, and a period of self-doubt and fear. But it also included a period of guidance, restoration of self-confidence, and a renewal of their faith and dependence on God.

The memorial of the stones became a part of Jewish history, in which they told and retold the story of their journey such that they would always remember from whence they had come.

As Black people in America celebrate Black History Month, our children, who reap the benefits of our forefathers' toil, will come and ask, "What means these programs?"

What means these programs that bombard us with never-ending nostalgic litanies of generations passed and circumstances long since changed?

What means these peculiar sounding old songs, with words that butcher the king's English like "Ain't and Dat and Gwine and Hebn?'"

-II-

What means these stones?

These occasions, like those stones set on the side of the riverbank, provide the veteran warriors an opportunity to tell the young who follow them that this has not been an easy road to walk.

These stones remind us of the following:

— As we sit down and order a hamburger in a restaurant that it was only a few years ago, hundreds of men and women were beaten and dragged from the same counter with their blood-soaked fingers clinging to the countertops as they stood up for the dream that one day Blacks folks could eat a whopper without getting a whopper on his head.

— When we sit in a classroom with the same facilities and opportunities as White children, that this was made possible to us by hundreds of Black men and women who put their lives on the line, dangled from the end of ropes, and painted the sidewalks with their blood that we might have a chance to learn our ABCs without the FBI and the KKK.

— When we go to the polls and cast a ballot, it is a privilege won for us by thousands who were burned in their homes, dragged from the back of wagons, and tortured to their deaths that we might have a right to build up with a ballot rather than tear down with a bullet.

I MADE IT

What means these stones?

For Israel, these stones represented the twelve tribes that made up the nation. These stones served as milestones to mark their progress on their journey.

There was a stone for Reuben, Simeon, Gad, Judah, Issachar, Zebulun, Manasseh, Ephraim, Benjamin, Dan Asher, and Naphtali. There was a stone for every son of Jacob.

When the children of Black America ask what means these stones, we should tell them that these programs represent the sum total of our aspirations and the totality of our being.

For Black, the twelve stones might take on a different meaning but no less significant.

The stones would represent the following:

— 1.–2. Our quest for freedom and liberty. No man can realize his full value and worth as a child of the Lord unless he is free to move about, think, and speak without unnecessary restraint.

— 3.–4. Our quest for equality and justice. We desire to see the day when the words of the Declaration of Independence are realized, "That all men are created equal and endowed by their creator with certain inalienable rights and among these are the right to life, liberty, and the pursuit of happiness."

— 5.–6. Our quest for education and excellence. The demand of our times is for the best and the brightest to take charge. We desire the best education our circumstances can acquire. We applaud the excellence of pursuit in every walk of life.

— 7.–8. The sum total of our cultural and artistic experience. We are Leontyne Price and Marian Anderson, but we are also Diana Ross and Marian Anderson. We are the pulpit dynamics of the Rev. CL Franklin, but we are also the master rap of Run-DMC. We are the syncopated Gospel sound of James Cleveland, but we are the simple chords of Lucy Campbell, who told us there is "something within." We are the blues of BB King, the jazz of Count Basie, the ragtime of Scott Joplin, and the mellow rock of Michael Jackson. These stones are our poets and writers, our actors and dreamers. They represent James Baldwin and Alex Haley, Phyllis Wheatley and Lorraine Hansbury, the sadness of Dunbar, and the dreams of Langston Hughes. These stones represent our cultural experiences, good or bad. What we have now has come as the result of a long journey.

— 9.–10. The sacrifices of our great leaders. No people have ever advanced without the sacrifice of men and women who rise to shoulder the responsibility of leadership. These stones help us to remember our leaders: Nat Turner, Frederick Douglas, Booker T. Washington, WEB DuBois, Marcus Garvey, Elijah Muhammad, A. Phillip Randolph, Adam Clayton Powell, Martin Luther King, Malcolm X, Stokely

I MADE IT

Carmicheal, and Jesse Jackson. These were men with varied views, methods, and opinions, but all men who stood up to our enemies and dared to sound the battle cry for freedom.

— 11.–12. Our dependence on the Lord. These stones mean that we have come a long way with the help of the Lord. You can't walk far without the help of the Lord! You can try as you will, but your journey won't get far without the Lord! Peter tried to walk a few steps atop the water but soon began to sink. He found that you can't walk far without the Lord! Somebody here is trying to begin a great undertaking, but you are trying to do it without the Lord! Somebody here is taking steps in a new direction, but you are trying to do it without the Lord. But when he found he was sinking, he called on the master, saying, "Lord! Lord! Save me!" Israel left Egypt on their own power, but after a little while, they soon realized that they could not go far without the Lord! After a while, they realized that without the Lord, there would be no food on their table! After a while, they realized that without the Lord, there would be clothes on their back or water when they were thirsty! Without the Lord, we could not make this journey alone! Don't you know that without the Lord, your room three-brick house could have been a one-room shanty? Or your three-room shotgun house could have been a cardboard box on the side of the street. Without

God, your one-finger push button Mercedes Bentz would be an outstretched thumb on the side of the road! No wonder the songwriter said, "Without God, I could do nothing, / without God, I'd surely fail, / without God, I would be drifting, like a ship without a sail!"

These stones tell the story:

— Of the rugged road we have traveled
— Of the sacrifices we have made
— Of our victories and our defeats
— Of our hopes and our dreams

But these stones are historical markers. They are not the end of the journey.

There is still:

— One more river to cross
— One more valley to span
— One more battle to fight
— One more enemy to defeat

I heard a songwriter say, "I don't feel no ways tired, / I've come too far from where I started from. / Nobody told me that the road would be easy, / I don't believe they brought me thus far just to leave me!"

STRANGE RUNNING BUDDIES

Scripture: "Wherein they think it strange that ye run not with them to the same excess of riot, speaking evil of you" (1 Peter 4:4).

INTRODUCTION

Have you ever been accused of being odd because you didn't go along with the crowd?

If you have, then you can relate to the two pigs that enjoyed themselves daily wallowing in the mud. They rolled in the mud. They napped in the mud. They had plenty of fun as they chased each other and played pig games in the mud. No matter how muddy one became, the other could always identify him. They knew each other well.

One day, the master selected one of the pigs to compete in the county fair. He washed the pig and rubbed him down. He tied ribbons around him and kept him meticulously clean. Several weeks later, the little pig left en route to the fair. He passed the trough and stopped to speak to his buddy.

"Come on in!" shouted his buddy. "It's good and messy! Let's roll around in the mud like we used to!"

The little pig looked at him and shook his hand. "I'm sorry. I can't do that anymore because I'm trying to win the prize for the master."

"You're not the same!" said the dirty pig. "You forgot what you are. You a pig just like me."

"You're right!" came the answer. "I'm just a pig that used to wallow in the mud. But I've been washed by the master's hand, and I'm on my way to claim my prize."

So it is with those who have decided to follow Christ. They have been washed in the blood of the lamb. They look strange to those they left behind, but they have found a new running buddy. They walk a new walk. They talk a new talk, and together, they are on their way to the promised land!

Many Christians have found Jesus to be a good friend. He is always there and will never let go. To those who don't understand the Christian life, having a best friend like Jesus could well be a "strange running buddy."

EXPOSITION

Peter, writing to Christians who were scattered around the world, urged them to be strong in the faith and to continue in the new life they had begun in Christ. He repeated his theme to them, although he knew they already knew it, for their memory's sake: Christians should not live by the flesh but by the spirit.

In verse 3, he lists six sins of the old life that should be abandoned by Christians living new lives in Christ: lasciviousness, lust, excesses of wine, revelings, banquetings, and abominable idolatries. Lasciviousness refers to all forms of lewd, vulgar, or impure behavior. Lusts refer to strong or overpowering sexual desires. Wine, banqueting, abominations, and revealing refer to drunkenness, wild parties, orgies, drinking matches, and other festivities where such things occur.

Peter reminded Christians that when they were in the world, they did such things, and their friends were people who invited them to and encouraged them to participate in these kinds of worldly activities.

In verse 5, however, he notes that Christians who have turned away from the world and have found new friendship with Christ and his followers are often scorned by their former running buddies because "they think it strange that ye run not with them to the excess of riot," and they start to speak evil of the Christian life. His encouragement to Christians in this circumstance is found in verse 7, "The end of all things is at hand, be ye therefore sober, and watch unto prayer."

Sleeping with hounds, running with rabbits

There are at least two occasions when a person can have a strange running buddy: when he leaves the world and turns to Christ and when he runs with the world while claiming a love for Christ. In either instance, people think his behavior is "strange."

When a convert comes to Christ, his old buddies think his new behavior is strange. He is no longer interested in worldly activities. His conversation has changed, and his motivation seems to be different. As compared to his former self, he is a strange and different person.

On the other hand, there are some who have claimed Christ as a friend and still run with the world at the same time. It's a case of "sleeping with the hounds and running with rabbits." Such persons send strange signals to their friends about the sincerity of their new friendship with Christ. They notice that these people preach, sing in the choir, serve as deacons, head church committees, usher, and otherwise work faithfully in the church. They sleep with the hounds. But what strikes them as strange is that some of these same people go to wild parties, drink alcohol, have affairs, have live-in lovers, and enjoy vulgar entertainment. They run with the rabbits.

Old buddies may think it strange if a Christian changes his life. But they think it's even stranger if the Christian claims a newborn-again life but still runs in his old circles.

Those who are in the church who still run with rabbits are, at best, confused and, at worse, hypocrites. Elijah challenged the people atop Mt. Carmel and asked, "How long halt ye between two opinions?" If God is God, follow him. If Baal is God, follow him. Joshua asked, "Who is on the Lord's side?" Jesus said, "No man can serve two masters because he will either hate the one and love the other, or he will love the one and hate the other." Those who try to walk with God and run with the devil at the same time have strange running buddies.

A true friend

While there are some who are utterly confused about the Christian life, those who really know the Lord have found him to be a true friend who sticketh closer than a brother. Our friendship with Christ accounts for why we have chosen to abandon the glitz and the flare of the world and have redirected our energies toward activities that are beneficial to God, family, and our fellow man.

The friendship we have with Christ is stronger than blood. All family members are not our friends. Cain and Abel were brothers from the same parentage, but Cain killed Abel. Jacob and Esau were brothers, yet they were enemies for nearly most of their lives, and their families feuded for centuries after them. The friendship we have found in Jesus is stronger than family ties. If family members think it's strange that we have found the Lord, then so be it.

Our friendship with Christ goes deeper than our deepest love. There are some husbands and wives who are our lovers but not our friends. Samson and Delilah were lovers, but they were not friends because Delilah used the weaknesses she knew about Samson and destroyed him. While husbands, wives, and lovers may forsake, we have found Jesus is always by our side.

Our friendship with Christ even goes beyond our strongest associations. All of those who run with you are not your friends. Job had three so-called friends who sat with him, gave him bad advice, and falsely accused him. Jesus had twelve so-called friends. One betrayed, another denied him three times, and the others abandoned him when the going got rough. While friends may forsake us, we have found that Jesus is always there.

Those who don't understand the Christian life say we have a "strange" running buddy.

We talk to a man that they cannot see, and they say that's strange. But if they knew Jesus, they would say. "Amazing Grace, how sweet the sound that saved a wretch like me. I once was lost, but now I'm found, blind, but now I see."

They think it's strange because we talk to the Lord, but I get a blessing when I talk to the Lord. No wonder the songwriter declared, "I come to the garden alone, while the dew is still on the roses, and the voice I hear, falling on my ear the son of God discloses. And he walks with me and he talks with me and he tells me I am his own and the joy we share as we tarry there, none other has ever known."

They think it's strange because we walk with the Lord, but our daily prayer is that the Lord will lead and guide us. I heard the songwriter declare, "Walk with me, Lord, walk with me! While I'm on this tedious journey, Lord, I want Jesus to walk with me."

They think it's strange that we depend so heavily on the Lord. We trust in the Lord because we never found the following:

— Battle that he could not win
— Burden that he could not lift

- Heartache that he could not heal
- Loneliness that he could not comfort
- Problem that he could not solve
- Mountain that he could not move

I have found a friend who has done the following:

- Conquered where others have failed
- Succeeded when others were defeated
- Been strong when others were weak
- Continued with me when others have given up

No wonder the saint declares, "What a friend we have in Jesus, / all our sins and grieves to bear! What a privilege to carry everything to God in prayer!"

This friend I have loves me so much that he took up an old rugged cross for me and carried me up!

Depending on Jesus

Text: Hebrews 12:1–2
Introduction

The Christian life may be compared to an Olympic race. We are instructed to strip off anything that slows us down or holds us back, especially sins that wrap themselves so tightly around our feet and trip us up. Running with patience, we must keep our eye on Jesus.

I. The Christian life is a race
    A. To enter, the contestant must qualify.
        1. The Olympic runner was required to subject himself to rigid training and tests to qualify physically. One with a weak heart or lungs could not enter.
        2. The Christian must meet the qualifications which are exacting and demanding. There is no excuse for one who fails.

B. Must lay aside every weight.
   1. Runners were stripped for the race. They did not run fully dressed, carrying a twenty-five-pound weight in each hand.
   2. No excess baggage when one runs this race.
   3. The sin (cf. Romans 6:6). It is the inherited depravity, and it must be cleansed (1 John 1:7, 9)

C. Looking unto King Jesus as you run. Keep your eyes upon the Lord, not on other people. He is the author and finisher of our faith.

II. Jesus is the author and finisher of our faith
   A. The source of our faith
      1. A gift from God (1 Corinthians 12:9) We are saved by faith (Ephesians 2:8–9) We live by Faith (Romans 10:7; Mark 9:29)
   B. Christ is the object of our faith. All life must be built around him. Do all to His glory. Illustration: This was the secret of Paul's life.
   C. The finisher of our faith. He perfects our life. He rewards our faith.

III. The example of our faith is Jesus
   A. He endured the cross, but His whole life was a cross with calvary as a climax.

B. He despised the shame. He rose above it; He mastered it.
   C. Exalted at the right hand of God.
   D. What a climax of faith the Christian is brought to.

Conclusion

We must look to Jesus Christ always. His eyes are upon us. It is a great opportunity to live and work for Jesus.

THE PRICE IS RIGHT

Scripture: "Ye are bought with a price, be not ye the servants of men" (1 Corinthians 7:23). "For as much as ye know that ye were not redeemed with corruptible things, as silver and gold, from your vain conversation received by tradition from your fathers, but with the precious blood of Christ as of a lamb without spot" (1 Peter 1:18–19).

INTRODUCTION

A popular television show which airs each day is *The Price Is Right.* On this program, contestants are given an opportunity to guess the price of a particular item. If they are successful, then they are able to claim the prize and take it home. Many wait each day to hear the announcer proclaim, "Come on down, you are the next contestant on the fabulous price is right." Persons who are familiar with the prices of goods usually have reasonable success in this show; others are not so successful.

The price of an object is the amount that is paid for the privilege of ownership. In the marketplace, the price of an object is determined by the cost of production and the amount of profit that the seller wants to make. Some items have a high price; others are lower.

Today, we are here to remind all who will listen that salvation is available for all. Its price is phenomenally low although its cost was extremely high. Any man or woman who will accept Christ will find that he can be forgiven of sin and given a new lease on life all by just for the asking.

THE COST OF SALVATION

Our text first considers the matter of cost. This text comes from the first Epistle of Peter, written to the church, reminding them that they were not their own but that they had been paid for by the Lord and Savior Jesus Christ.

The idea of redemption was first introduced in the twenty-fifth chapter of Leviticus, in which God related special rules by which people could redeem what had been lost. Under the Mosaic law, if a man had lost his property, he could pay a price and redeem it. If a poor man who had no income lost that which was his, his family was allowed to pay the price and redeem it. If a man had been sold into slavery, his relatives or others could come in and pay the price and redeem. The payment for redemption was usually in gold or silver. Cash money was required.

In the case of a slave, if he was redeemed and the price was paid, that slave became the property of his new master. They obeyed his commands, moved in his direction, and were obligated through loyalty to their new master.

Peter, in this Epistle, projected to the church that we who had lost the privilege of heaven…we who had lost the claim to the celestial heights…we whose transgressions of the law had closed forever behind us the opportunity to enter into gold-paved streets of paradise…we who because of our own fleshly weakness have lost our claim to eternal life…we who because of our sometimes unwitting allegiance to Satanic powers have given way to evil in our lives…we who were lost have been redeemed! And we were redeemed with a price.

Now there was a cost for this redemption. There was a cost for this redemption.

Peter notes in the passage that unlike the redemption of property and slaves in Old Testament times, the cost for the redemption of our souls could not be paid in silver and gold. The cost had to be paid by the shedding of blood.

That requirement is not unusual when we consider that the law required that the remission of sin could only come with the shedding of blood. There was blood of varied kinds. Certain sins required the death of certain kinds of animals, goats for one sin and doves for another, etc. Therefore, if someone was attempting to redeem those who were lost to sin, he would have to redeem those who were lost to sin he would have to redeem in accordance with the requirements of the law. He would have to redeem it with the shedding of blood.

Brothers and sisters, I suggest to you that at one time, we were lost in sin. I suggest to you that we have transgressed the mighty laws of God. I suggest that in any given week or day, we have done many wrong things in the eyesight of God. But we have a special joy in knowing that despite the wretchedness of our estate, one Jesus looked at the requirements of the law and decided to pay the price.

The cost of salvation would not be a low cost, but one that was extremely high.

The cost of salvation would not be as simple as paying silver and gold. If it were that simple, that would be no problem for the Lord of the universe, for the rocks and the hills could be ordered to compress themselves in such a way that they would produce gold and silver in amounts of silver to redeem all who desire to be saved. Gold and silver would not pose a problem for the Lord of the universe because "my father is rich in houses and land, and he holds the wealth of the world in his hand."

The cost of salvation could not be so simple as providing precious stones, for the Lord of the universe has access to rubies and diamonds. They come so freely that John said he saw them in such abundance that the holy city was adorned with them. He saw twelve gates to the city, and each was made of giant pearls. He said he saw a city that was sitting on twelve foundations, and each of the foundations was sitting on precious stones. He saw stones of jasper and sapphires, topaz, emeralds, and precious stones decorated the holy city and seemed to be freely available everywhere. But the price that had to be paid for redemption could not be paid in precious stones, for the law required that redemption of sin had to be paid with the shedding of blood.

The cost of salvation had to be paid on demand and could not be charged to the heavenly master charge and paid in monthly installments.

I MADE IT

THE HEAVENLY EXPRESS CARD

Some have access to an abundance of charge cards such as Visa, Master Card, and American Express. These cards help us to cushion the high cost of a product by spreading out the payments over an extended period.

It's good to have access to an American Express card. It lets the world know that you are in good standing, and your purchase will be backed up by the strength of American Express. Often, we can get the things we want by simply putting them on the card.

But while it's good to have an American Express card, we need to be concerned about our heavenly express card. The heavenly card bears the name of an individual who is in good standing with the bank of heaven.

The heavenly express card is recognized in all sections of the world.

The heavenly express card can get you things that you cannot receive under ordinary circumstances.

Hezekiah found that when his life was running out on him, the Lord allowed him to charge fifteen more years on his heavenly express card.

A poor widow woman one day discovered that when the food in her barrel was running low, the Lord fixed it such that she could charge meal and oil on her heavenly express card, and her barrel never ran out, though she used it day by day.

Somebody here today has been living from day to day, backed up by the grace of God. By the standards of men, you should have run out a long time ago. But your heavenly express card brought bread down from heaven and blessing beyond measure.

In the Garden of Gethsemane, Jesus pondered a way that he might be able to pay the cost of redemption without paying the price of Calvary. Maybe he could charge redemption's price against his account in heaven. But that could not be done because the law required that blood had to be paid and paid on demand. Jesus would have to go all the way to pay the price.

The cost of salvation was payable only with the blood.

The cost of salvation was payable only with the life of the lamb.

The cost of salvation would require the sacrifice of life and lamb.

The cost of salvation would require the Lamb of God to lay himself on the altar and be the sacrifice that would redeem lost men and women.

Sometimes, I ask the question, "Was it for crimes that I have done that he hung out on a tree with nails in his hands? Was it for crimes that I have done that the blood poured from his side, that he dropped his head and died?"

Jesus paid the cost of salvation, and Peter said it was not paid in silver and gold. It was not paid in negotiable savings bonds. It was not paid in money market certificates. It was not paid in exchange for property of collateral assets. But it was paid through the precious blood of Jesus.

Paid that we might have a chance to everlasting life.

A song writer said, "Jesus paid it all, / all to him I owe. Sin had left a crimson stain, / but he washed it white as snow."

THE PRICE OF SALVATION

Finally, brothers and sisters, it's nice to know the cost of salvation, but what about the selling price?

In the marketplace, when something has a high production cost, it usually has a high selling price. If it costs a lot to make it, you expect to pay a high price in the marketplace.

Well, here is salvation. It has a high cost, and somebody here perhaps thought that I wouldn't be able to pay the price. Somebody here is thinking that the cost of salvation was so high that it required the Son of God, the Lily of Valley, to die on the cross…the cost is so high that I won't be able to pay it.

Though there was a high cost for salvation, it had a very low price.

When something is on sale, that means that it is being offered at a reduced price. When something is a bargain, that means it is considerably lower than the selling price. You might find bargains, but you won't find a place where you get products absolutely free.

The price tag of salvation reads absolutely free. Jesus paid it all. I suggest to you that the price is right.

The price tag for entrance into the kingdom of heaven is absolutely free. I suggest to you that the price is right!

The price tag to enter the celestial realms is absolutely free. I suggest to you that the price is right!

If It's Not One Thing, It's Another

---

2 Corinthians 8:2

How that in a great trial of affliction, the abundance of their joy and their deep poverty abounded unto the riches of their liberality?

Yes, we are led by and for a paradoxical purpose and ideals, and this is just one of the many scriptures that bear us out that we are a paradoxical people.

To say that we live in a bewildered and transistorized world is to put it mildly, for we are constantly being rejected from one degree of things or from one thing of another, and therefore, we foster the idea and plant upon every lip the phrase, "If it's not one thing, it's another."

Some of these things are good, and some are bad, but what drives us to these distractions mostly are the adverse conditions that are threatening our most placid position.

The great writer, orator, and preacher Timothy Dwight has said, "Human life is ordinarily nothing less than a collection of disappointments."

Due to the fact that God has set up a divine plan, inherently, we try to bypass this plan and propose a plan of our own, but our plans are forever being revamped, if not completely discarded.

VOCATION WISE

We seek to be a farmer and end up becoming a mechanic. Likewise, he, who sought to be a lawyer, ended up being a doctor.

He who pursued the role of a merchant seaman ends up a preacher. And on and on the story goes. The mind is subjected to great anticipation and greater disappointment, for the principle design of the mind in laboring for these things is to become superior to others. But almost all rich men are brought to grips with the grim reality that there are others who are much richer than themselves.

Even the successful competitor in the race utterly misses his aim. The real enjoyment existed, although it was unperceived only by contending languish for want of competition, and we utter in disgust, "If it's not one thing, it's another."

There are two modes in which we seek happiness in the enjoyment of the present world.

Most persons truly indulge their wishes and intend to find objects sufficient in number and value to satisfy them. A few aim at satisfaction by proportioning their desire to the number and measures of their probable gratifications. But how to be disappointed and desires let loose, only to terminate is distress. The child cries for a toy; the moment he gets it, he throws it down and cries for another, and this act is repeated over and over until he or she has a pile in a heap. He looks at them disdainfully and leaves them without regret.

Men are merely taller children. Honor, wealth, and splendor are the toys for which grown children pine, but which, however, accumulate, leave them still disappointed and unhappy for their charging; they find, "If it's not one thing, it's another."

Let us end our philosophical journey and take a short trip down the lane of the present.

We are confronted with problem after problem—war, demonstration, peace demonstrations, riots, protesting, religious relics, discrimination, integration, school busing, school nonbusing, jobs, overpopulation, dope, and poverty.

Yes, "If it's not one thing, it's another." As soon as one problem is solved, there are two to take its place.

By the time the car is paid for, you need a new motor. If it's not a set of new tires, it's the brakes that need replacing. If it's not the transmission, it's the wheels that need alignment. If it's not the car, it's the house. If it's not the roof, then the termites are eating the foundation away. By the time we pay taxes, the insurance is due. If it's not the heating unit, it's the air conditioner. If it's not the paint, it's the plumbing. "If it's not one thing, it's another." Even the elements of nature get in the act.

> If it's not too hot, it's too
> cold. If it's not knowing, it's
> raining. If it's not one thing,
> it's another.

Then there are our physical conditions.
If it's not your eyesight, it's your hearing.
If it's not your lungs, it's your kidneys.

If it's not your hair falling out, it's your teeth that need fixing. If it's not your back that's hurting, your feet are giving you trouble. If it's not an internal rash, it's an external rash. If it's not too much weight, it's not enough weight. If it's not arthritis that stops you from walking, it's laryngitis that stops you from talking. If I don't have a cold, I'm burning up with a fever. "If it's not one thing, it's another."

But we find that all conditions hinge upon our state of mind, for most of these conditions that we refer to as adverse are really things that we pray for at one time or the other; therefore, we should teach ourselves to be contented in whatever situation we find ourselves in.

Moderated desires constitute a character fitted to acquire all the good that this world can afford. The person who has found, even to some degree, to be contented in whatever situation he finds himself has learned effectively the art of being happy and possesses the alchemic stone.

Our text teaches us irresistibly that since you cannot command gratification, we should command our desires, and as the events of life do not accord with your wishes, your wishes should accord with them. For as life parades itself across the stage, "known as the land of the living," our minds are propelled into a frenzy with great expectation and anticipation as we rise and fall in and upon our faith.

Jesus, the great mind emancipator, has given us greater hope, for He has set before us an open door which is greater than wealth and even greater than the honor of all the Caesars. We can choose to spend eternity in hell with perpetual damnation, or we can wrap ourselves in the divine essence of the Almighty God and go home with him and live in joy, peace, and tranquility throughout eternal ages.

Yes, we live in a world that is a victim of "one thing or another," but if we live in and for Jesus, it will get sweeter and sweeter as the days go by.

And one day soon, we will be able to lay aside all paradoxical situations and ideas.

> For every crooked way will be straight,
> Every mountain will be made level,
> Every valley will be filled.

CHRIST'S CONSTRAINETH LOVE

2 Corinthians 6:11–13

Paul's second letter to the Corinthians deals with practical and speculative difficulties, answering inquiries and correcting the abuses of unsatisfactory churches. This epistle is the impassioned self-defense of a wounded spirit against erroring and ungrateful people. The predominant word in this book is affliction. Yet Christ himself stands out in love and blessings. Paul here is representing the savior's love. It is not merely something to be admired only but enjoyed as something that acts as a spiritual force. Paul experienced love as the supreme power over his own life. He had confidence in the principles of love, which renew and bless the world. (ver.)

Some may interpret this verse as a subjective genitive, which means Christ's love for man. Others may interpret it as the objective genitive, which means our love for Christ. But constraineth love interfuses each other. Jesus loved us first, and we should love him because the constraining influence of Christ's love was a relinquishment of heavenly glory. He exchanged the highest place above for one of the lowest on earth. The most striking proof of his love is the comprehensive range within (which his love operates) (Psalm 139:7–9).

His acts of kindness, his love for his friends, his painful death, physically, mentally, and spiritually (and the object of his death) were redemption, purification, exaltation, and eternal happiness for men. Let us not forget to consider the prayer he offered for his enemies while they nailed him to the cross (Luke 23:34). Love forgives, love exalts, love purifies, it does more than talk (Matthew 5:43). When we were yet sinners, Christ died for us. And now He is at the right hand of His Father, making intercession for us. (Christ's constraineth love cannot be denied.) It is not a secret; love is seen (Hebrews 7:25).

Christ's love constrained Paul. His love compressed Paul's irresistible power. Then all of Paul's energies went into one channel (for the love and glory of god). Those who put all of their love into one channel are not so easy to run out. Those who once loved God and are not loving Him now have too many channels to put their love in (it's run out). Men don't love God or the church. The Bible is just another book. If you tell men about the church, they believe everybody is after no good in church. They have the sense to hate and no wisdom to love (they are easy to be influenced) and constrain various motives. Some are low, and some are high (but constraineth love is of Jesus Christ).

Nowadays, man's natural instinct and impulse is to regard public opinion. It matters not how low, immoral, or irreligious it may be (men love public opinion). Public opinion has more power to draw them than God's word. Most men have more ambition and energy to boost the devil's program than they do God's. They can party all night without getting exhausted, restless, or impatient. (theme)

Love takes control of the best as well as the worst. Troubles won't stop it from acting. It seems like most people are against leading a life of love. Most of them are too busy introducing conflicts and making enemies. Rebelling and hating and keeping a disturbance going. No man is born to engage in such a life. It is morally wrong to use people selfishly to make yourself happy. Some just can't be happy and don't feel successful working with others.

You may find a job where you think you won't have to mix with others, but sooner or later, you will run into loneliness. Seldom can any man do a job well alone. If you go on a vacation, you will need the cooperation of others. Cooperation with others will make a greater chance for success and satisfaction. And by the same token, you can help others. And have a happier life yourself. (Keep on loving; it pays off in the end.)

Interested. A Christian should not be too selfish to show genuine concern. Love looks for good things in others, and when you find it, don't be afraid to make it known. You won't lose anything. It's important for people to love. But it is bad to let anyone see you with one face on in a crowd and another face on behind their backs. (Without the spirit of love, you will never be outstanding.)

I am not teaching you to be a politician, but I am saying, "Get down to what life really is all about. Love others as yourself. Try to get to know others and fellowship with others. Love will loosen up tight dispositions." How can we love God, whom we have never seen, and hate your brother? (1 John 3:14).

Jesus went about doing good; every sickness he healed. Every demon he expelled and every sinner he pardoned. And that's not all. He is sympathetic and tender. He is forbearing and patient. (Oh, how I love Jesus.) Nothing can make people want to be loved more than anything else. They want to feel you are separating me from his love. The love of God constraineth us.

Love is a sky of unknown dimensions. No flying machine can reach its heights. Love is an unexplored distance. No tape can measure its length. Love is a bridge over deep water. Lord, help me to live from day to day. Even when I kneel to pray, Lord, let my prayer be for others.

Help me in all my work to ever be sincere and true. I can't stop loving God. Love renews, strengthens, and controls.

Many complain that church holds too long, the choir sings too long, and want the preacher to rush through his sermon (because they have other things to do). Let me admonish you, anything you feel the most obligated to do has the biggest grip on you. Only a few have the constraineth love of Christ.

Man has neglected God, disrespected mothers and fathers, and forsaken his brother and sister and others (no love). Physical power is of two kinds. It's either energy or resistance. You see, a ship cannot sail on an artificial ocean. A gun is nothing without bullets. And steam engines are

I MADE IT

no good without steam. Everything works with the help of another object. So it is with life that you cannot stop indulging in worldliness and others' sins until you have been delivered by God's divine power. You cannot love until you have been born by God's spirit. (When we love) (Romans 8:28) no love (Luke 6:39) (theme).

Many don't have time for love because they are trying to get to the top (but there is no top). If you had fifty million dollars, you would want sixty million. It's good to put some value on the dollar, but there are other things to think about. Your family: wife, husband, children, but most of all, salvation for the soul, and gratitude to God and his love for you). That means more than trying to get to the top.

When you join the rat race, you have already lost. Some make thousands of dollars a week, and some make fifty. (They both are in the rat race.) If your job does not include time for God, relaxation, and enjoyment, it's not worth having. If you spend all your time making a living and never have time for really living, you are as good as dead.

And if you are the worrying kind, you better leave management alone. (Get out of the rat race). And live unto Christ (Galatians. 3:20) (theme)

In verse 1, the love of Christ should be so much a part of you until you become a new creation. The old life of sin is forgotten, and the life which you have risen into is a life of righteousness. There is a greater power operating upon you than the power of self. The word constrain means that it keeps us irresistible to object. In this, it shows that love is stronger than death. No man can love until he becomes a new creature in Christ.

Constraining love is manifested in a Christian spirit because a Christian has the spirit of peace. In fact, every good man is a peacemaker. By character, disposition, and active efforts, love makes and composes differences and promotes harmony among men. Love keeps us in line with moral rules, divine law, and authoritativeness. Love constrains speech with a soft answer. Love seasons speech with grace. Love, control act, and plans for the best when men lie to you and set traps to hurt you.

Continue in love, in spite of obstacles or oppositions. We never dream that we are in trouble until we are trapped (Isaiah 40:31) (theme).

Let us guard ourselves from mistakes. Some think they are flying emotionally. Flying depends absolutely on surrender and trust. (Can you fly today?) Those who fly on spiritual wings don't knock down and walk on others. Or stir up bitterness and strife in the church. Our soul was made to live in the upper atmosphere and not in strife.

I want to close with a story about those who were having domestic problems. One had an atheist for a husband. One had a gambler, and the third one had a drunkard. They were traveling on a long journey. Finally, they came to the end of the road, and they began asking one another, "How are we going across the mountain?"

The first one said, "I believe I will stay here and tunnel through the mountain."

Some people won't help themselves or ask God to help their helplessness. They just make themselves satisfied, staying in the same old place.

The second woman said, "I believe I will walk around the mountain because I don't want to spread my wings." The third woman said, "I know what I'm going to do. I'm going to mount up on my wings and fly over the mountain. We have to spread our wings."

When they are greatly emotional, flying is a matter of principle, and not life is just like the life of an eagle's nest. When the mother eagle wants the young eagle to rise up on the pension of their wings, she scratches some of the comforts out of the nest to make them rise up on their wings. God has to do that to us sometimes. Sometimes, it takes rising above trials, snares, and troubles in the spirit of love, by the spirit of pureness, by knowledge, by long-suffering, by kindness, by the holy ghost, and by love unfeigned. Sometimes, it takes spreading our wings of trust, faith, and hope to cross the mountains of life's difficulties. (difference and indifference). Constraineth love maketh one want to be a part of Jesus and the church.

A captain lay on a Western battlefield at Shiloh. He suffered a fatal gunshot. In pain and thirsty, he lay, looking at the beautiful stars which shone above the dark battlefield. He said, "The God who hung those stars gave his son on Calvary's cross for me one day. And since I'm going where he is one day, even though I'm wounded on a dark battlefield, I can praise my God while I'm suffering."

Coke Is the Real Thing

Scripture: "Let us hear the conclusion of the whole matter: Fear God and Keep his commandments: for this is the whole duty of man?" (Ecclesiastes 12:13).

INTRODUCTION

Madison Avenue in New York is the home of many of the world's greatest advertising agencies. From these offices spring a varied conglomeration of jungles and slogans that have tickled the ears and hearts of America for generations.

Some of the advertising slogans of Madison Avenue that have caught the imagination of millions of Americans have been those prepared for the Coca-Cola Company. Some of these slogans have included the following: "Things go better with Coke," "Coke adds life to," "Coke is it," and the most famous of them all, "Coke is the real thing."

The real thing. There are millions in the world today who are searching for it and have never found it. The Coke Company captured that quest in a slogan and made millions of dollars. Our Lord has an answer today for those who are in search of the real thing, and it's in his Word.

–I–
Solomon Searched for the Real Thing

Our text first considers that Solomon searched the entirety of his life for ultimate happiness…or the real thing. The book of Ecclesiastes is a record of his search and the endeavors he undertook to achieve ultimate happiness.

Chapter after chapter of this book is filled with lists of undertakings that Solomon pursued in his quest for the real thing.

He studied nature, the sun, the moon, the stars, the rivers, and streams, but he concluded that this, too, was vanity…is not the real thing. He pursued building projects, feeling that upon their completion, he would achieve total happiness. So he built the great temple of the Lord, palaces, great gardens, and pools. But in all of his building and architectural genius, he concluded that this, too, is vanity…it is not the real thing.

He even pursued doing nothing; he resolved that there is a time for everything under the sun, a time to be born and a time to die, a time to laugh and a time to cry, and he resolved that perhaps there was a time for him just to do nothing. He also pursued the accumulation of riches, placed heavy taxes on his people, and became one of the richest kings the world has ever known. Moreover, he chased women for happiness. He married three hundred women and maintained seven hundred girlfriends on the side. He undertook an appreciation of good music, hosting many social gatherings and parties on such a grand scale that they could not be equaled.

But even a free-thinking, non-infringing lifestyle could not bring him true happiness. Even the accumulation of great riches, the cheering presence of friends at an endless string of parties, or the warming passions of Israel's most beautiful maidens could not bring him happiness. "She resolved that it was all vanity. It is not the real thing."

There are many today, like Solomon, who are trying a variety of endeavors, trying to find happiness, but to no avail. Some are seeking happiness in scholarship, in the persistent pursuit of pleasure and good times, in chasing members of the opposite sex, and some of us have charted a course of upward mobility targeted to riches and fame, while others have decided to live a life of lazy existence.

Solomon concluded that the resolution of the quest for happiness should be that we "fear God and keep his commandments for that is the whole duty of man."

One songwriter said, "Only what you do for Christ will last. Only what you do for Christ will last."

–II–
COKE Is the Real Thing

Finally, brothers and sisters, Solomon took a lifetime to find the meaning of the real thing. He wasted valuable years of his life chasing empty visions, mirages, and empty pursuits. Only at the close of his life did he discover that the only real things in life are associated with God.

Money is not the real thing, but God is everlasting.

Sex is not the real thing, but God is eternal.

Fame is not the real thing, but God is universal.

Every Christian knows that the things of this world are tangible and fleeting, but if we give our lives to Christ and "Seek ye first the kingdom of heaven and its righteousness," all the other things will be added.

Christ is the real thing.

The letters of the word COKE spell it out for the world: C–hrist O–our K–ing E–ternal is the real thing.

If we could go to Madison Avenue in New York, we could write some commercials that could tell of our love for Christ. Our commercials would tell the world that we seek Christ in everything.

Jesus is like Coke…he is the real thing.

Jesus is like Coke…he adds life to everything we do.

Jesus is like Coke…things go better with Jesus.

Jesus is like Coke… Christ is it!

Jesus is like Quaker State…he keeps you running strong.

Jesus is like All State…with Jesus, you're in good hands.

Jesus is like EF Hutton…when he speaks, the world listens.

Jesus is like Texaco…he's the man behind the stars.

Jesus is like Ford…he's got a better idea.

Jesus is like BC Powder…he makes you come back strong.

Jesus is like Geritol…he's good for saving poor blood.

Jesus is like Prudential…he's the rock of the ages.

Jesus is like Tony Tiger… he's g–r–e–a–t, great!

Jesus is like Eveready batteries…he's got power to spare.

Jesus is like Budweiser…when you say Jesus, you've said it all.

Jesus is like Rolaids…his name spells relief.

Jesus, our Lord, is the real thing. Before him, every knee shall bow, and every tongue confesses that he is the Lord of Lords.

IF YOU NEED IT, GOD GOT IT

Matthew 7:7

These clauses mark the climatic challenge of the three steps. Ask, seek, and knock, which this verse contains. The Bible reveals God long before it occurred or man had the wit to turn to him. While man was still in darkness and shrunk in sin, God took the initiative to rise from His throne. God lays aside His glory and stoops to seek man until He finds him before man stirs himself to seek God. We do not see man groping after God in the Bible. We see God reaching for man by taking the initiative to create man holy. No man can visualize God sitting comfortably on a distant throne, uninterested and indifferent to moral needs. He rather extends a universal invitation to all mankind. Life is a sheet of paper on which we all can write a line or two to our maker (Matthew 7:7) (theme).

If God has spoken and acted, He gave in His noblest act of redemption to the world (through Jesus.) We must not only wish for forgiveness for sin. We must cry out and beg for pardon for sin because, for this cause, he came. The first word in the text permits us to ask. But the world has some admiration for that (ask.) But the largest part of humanity despises the (ask) system. They respect those who are plenteous and hate the poor. No earthly father can extend such an invitation and fulfill it as God. The earthly father may not give his children a stone for bread or a scorpion for a fish. But his givings are limited. (This is not so with God.) Ask what you will in His name so long as you are from God.

We have heard that if you make one step, God will make two. But according to the text, God has already made three steps: ask, seek, and knock. For behind every petition in the text, God has promised to fulfill. Behind our asking, it shall be given to you. If we seeketh, we shall findeth. Behind our knock, it shall be opened unto us. This world in which we live is filled with diminishing and deceptiveness. But God is saying to us here if you need. Progress, the Lord has it. If you need peace, the Lord has it. If you need happiness, the Lord has it. We only have one command, and that is to ask. If you are bulked by difficulties, incidents, and individuality, a peculiarity of character, with untraceable habits and evil impulses. Ask God for a resurrection for the soul. If you have faith and ask in honesty, it shall be done. Ask him to let you walk with him and tell you to hate secrets for help to in-toil strains and frets. (theme)

The more asking means we have run into extremity, and perpetual asking means we have lost self-respect. Some people are too proud to ask God for their needs. Just make sure you need what you're asking. Many times, we ask for stones, scorpions, and earthly hindrances, which may tempt us to fall into sin or the stain of death, which weighs our heavenward journey. You should ask God every day of your life for the good path and the way to Zion and for salvation for your soul. But you be sure you need what you ask for.

The second step, Jesus told us, was to *seek,* which is to say. There is something lost or hidden. The shepherd searched for the lost sheep until he found him. So did God. He searched for lost souls. But the time has come for man to seek. We are to seek. Where shall we start our search? It is to begin with Jesus. Whose foundation the Christian religion is built upon? Christianity is not pious talk. It is not a collection of religious ideas. It is not a catalog of rules or an investigation of man. Christianity is a declaration of what God has done in Christ for human beings like ourselves. Christianity is a religion of salvation. And there is nothing in other religions that can compare with it. If you are ready to be saved, seek God. He is the author and finisher of faith (Hebrews 12:2, 2 Corinthians 12:9) (theme). The battle calls for strength.

Man is an insatiably inquisitive creature. He has a restless mind. He is always prowling into the unknown. He pursues knowledge with restless energy. His life is a voyage of discovery by questioning. Exploring, investigating, and researching, he never grows out of his child interminable. He is presuppositious when he approaches the Bible. He is unprepared to believe the Bible, and he won't allow God to convince his will. He maintains his opinion against God. But after he has found everything he searched for materially, he still lacks everything. Man will never find God by seeking God with his wisdom. He must seek God through His Word. With not only a humble mind but an open mind. And for those who find him, not only does he reverse their ideas. He reformed their entire lives, and those who have found Christ must be willing to lay aside a few things.

Lay aside prejudice and those hardened ways you are set in. Lay aside evil commotion, self-praising, self-pleasing, moral rebellion, slothfulness, laziness, and disobedience to God. Doing this may involve rethinking the whole outlook of life (2 Corinthians 5:17) (theme). God is unchangeable. So man must change to get support from God. Whatsoever you need, God's got it, but it is given under a manner of condition. (theme) Those who find Christ find readjustment in their manner of life from hesitating to do good. When you find Christ, you can communicate with other folk. Those who have found the man are not easily led by the crowd. No Christian has to swim the stream of the world to live. The path of the world is wide, and it has many travelers. It has the rich and the poor. It has the learned and ignorant. And they all have forgotten to let the will of the Lord be done in their lives (Matthew 5:20, Luke 12:__, Amo_ 5:24). Those who have found Christ seek his way. The way to get up is to get down. The way to receive is to give. The way to be exalted is to be abased. The way to be a master is to be a servant. The way to be wise is to be a fool for God. (theme)

God did not create us as horses or mules without an understanding. He gave us a mind. It's a mighty good time to use it. When you seek Christ, you are not seeking fun or an amusing pastime. This is a serious business. It's affecting our present way of living, and our future is destiny. If you seek God, you can find Him. He is not playing in a trackless jungle. Man is a sad picture today. Most men are seeking for riches and fame, industry promotion, and silver as a hidden treasure. I want to tell you today you must seek God with energy. (theme)

The third step: Jesus told us to knock, and a door will be opened unto us. There is a power on the other side, to fulfill all unconditional and unlimited promises. Knock when your needs are urgent. He will open if you knock. No sinner is too vile; knock. Jacob knocked when He wrestled with him until the break of day, and He changed his name. Solomon knocked, and He gave him wisdom, knowledge, and riches.

David knocked, and He gave him a clean heart and renewed his spirit. Hezekiah knocked, and He extended fifteen years on his life. Job knocked, and He gave him the patience to wait until his change came. Peter knocked, and He increased his faith. Paul knocked, and He gave him a crown of righteousness. Men are knocking every minute of the day. If you need a hiding place, God's got that too. Just knock. It doesn't get too late to knock on the Lord's door. And He is not too busy to answer the door. He opens. He owns the house. He is the architect. He is the landlord. He built the door.

God is the master. He owns the door. He has the key to the doors. Anywhere and anytime, He is still opening doors. Keep on knocking. Go down on your knees. You stay there and call Him sincerely from your heart. He may not come when you think he ought to come, but He is never late. Just keep on knocking.

Keep on knocking in the hour of trouble. Keep on knocking when the problem is too hard. Just keep on knocking. Anytime and anywhere. Keep on knocking, keep on knocking. Keep on knocking if you need it. God got it. Keep on knocking. Keep on knocking.

My Grace Is Sufficient

---·—⋄—·---

Scripture: "And he said unto me, My grace is sufficient for thee: for my strength is made perfect in weakness. Most gladly therefore will I rather glory in my infirmities, that the power of Christ may rest upon me" (2 Corinthians 12–9).

INTRODUCTION

Have you ever felt drained and worn out? Have you ever felt like you just could not go on? If so, then you can probably relate to the story of the pilgrim in the wilderness. A pilgrim, so the story goes, was on his journey home, traveled through beautiful green valleys, and rested in the cool of the day. But after a while, his journey carried him through the desert, which was without water, shade, or even a cool breeze. Soon he began to thirst, and he cried out to God, "Lord, I'm thirsty. Help me find water."

In response, he heard the Lord reply, "My grace is sufficient." God led him to a pile of rocks and told him to pick up one and carry it.

Troubled by the additional burden, the traveler called out to God, "Lord, I'm thirsty!"

Again, his answer was "My grace is sufficient." God showed him a large dried gourd and told him to carry it. Nearly exhausted, the pilgrim carried the rock and the gourd, frustrated with God.

"I asked for water, and he made my load heavier by adding a rock. I asked again, and all he gave me was an empty gourd."

Under the cover of night, the pilgrim stopped and rested against what appeared to be a large tree. He cried out to God that he could not go on. As he closed his eyes, completely drained, God's response was the same "My grace is sufficient for thee."

When the pilgrim opened his eyes the next morning, he was lying against a great cactus bulging with juices. God said, "Take the rock and cut the cactus. Take the gourd and catch the juices as they flow. When you have finished, fill your gourd, and it will be enough to carry you home."

The pilgrim gave thanks to God and rejoiced, for truly God's grace was sufficient for his need.

As Christians, we feel drained at times because we are human. It appears that instead of getting lighter, our load gets heavier. Sometimes, we are frustrated because the help we ask God for only seems to bring additional burdens. These are frustrating moments. But it's in moments like these that we should remember that God supplies our needs as we need them. If we continue to obey him, he will prove to us that his grace is sufficient for us to have life and have it more abundantly.

I MADE IT

EXPOSITION

This text considers the Apostle Paul as he writes his second Epistle to the Corinthians. It addresses a peculiar moment in his life when he was frequently frustrated by what he called a "thorn in the flesh." There are two schools of thought with respect to his thorn in the flesh. One holds that it referred to the presence of a physical illness that made his ministry more difficult. This school of thought suggests that the illness is chronic ophthalmia, a disease of the eyes. It was not extremely painful, but it made him repulsive in appearance. He referred to this illness in Galatians 4:13–15 and thanked the Galatians for tolerating his presence, which must have been troubling to gaze upon. The second school of thought suggests that the "thorn" was not an illness but the presence of a "messenger of Satan" who followed him everywhere he went. It focuses on the word "messenger" from the Greek word "aggelos," which means "angel of Satan." This school supposes that Paul believed that the troubles he faced in town after town were caused by this "messenger," which was a "thorn in his flesh." Whichever of the theories is correct, they both have one thing in common: they point out that Paul was frustrated by something that made his work for God difficult. On three different occasions, he asked God to remove the thorn, but God's answer was always the same, "My grace is sufficient." It appeared that the more he asked, the more troubles kept coming, and always the response from God was "My Grace is sufficient for thee."

Paul concluded that God had a good purpose in his actions because the constant frustrations that he felt kept him humble when it would have been easy to be caught up in pride. In his weakness, he wrote in verse 9 that he became whole or complete. He resolved to glory in his frustrations, knowing that if he did not give up, the glory of God would eventually rest upon him and give him victory.

THREE THORNS

Today, there are many like Paul who are trying to live the Christian life but are troubled by a messenger of Satan, which acts as a thorn in their flesh. Even the strongest Christian has experienced the presence of this thorn. Consider the various kinds of thorns:

- Economic thorns: There are some who are trying to live a Christian life, but they can never seem to get their finances in order. They try to save, and something depletes their savings. Expenses keep mounting: household appliances break, the car won't run, and the children need new shoes. Financial problems follow many of us around like a magnetic cloud. We worry so much about our finances that we can't think straight enough to talk to God effectively. Like Paul, who asked for the removal of his thorns, we have begged the Lord, on more occasions than one, to remove this thorn, but it remains. After asking the Lord to remove it three times, Paul considered his thorn had never stopped him from accomplishing what he set out to do, but it was humbling. In dealing with our finances, perhaps God is allowing us to accumulate just enough to keep us humble, knowing what we would do if we had more.

- Social thorns: there are many who live as Christians despite the frustrations we face in the community of men. Race discrimination, class differences, social injustice, and police brutality are just a few of the thorns that collectively affect many Christians as they try to live for God. Life would be much easier if we did not have to face these unfavorable conditions daily. They make our relations with men more difficult, and they make it hard to be a Christian. Like Paul, we as a people have asked for their removal, but they still exist. In hindsight, the very presence of these social thorns helps us to remember who we are and what others really think of us. We continue to progress as a people, but these thorns tend to keep us humble, lest we forget our African ancestry and roots in the Black American community.
- Personal thorns: These thorns involve our health and emotions. There are some of us who do well for the Lord but feel we could do much more if we were not plagued by ill health personally or in our family. Sickness slows our pace. At times, it drains our energy. We could do so much more without its presence, likewise with our loves and enemies. Problems in courtship and marriage seem

to plague some Christians and follow them from year to year. Others are always plagued by enemies who twist their words, misinterpret their deeds, and impute bad motives in their actions. It is at least frustrating. How many times have Christians prayed for the removal of such thorns, but yet they seem to persist? Paul's answer here is that they keep us weak or, in other words, humble. They serve a purpose, which is to our good, for "all things work together for the good of them that love the Lord, according to his purpose."

ENOUGH GRACE FOR OUR NEEDS

God's response to Paul was His grace was sufficient. When God says, "My grace is sufficient," he means that he gives us blessings and assistance in proportion to our daily needs and in proportion to our ability to handle it.

Israel complained to God that there was no bread, so God's grace rained down bread from heaven. But it was only enough grace to carry them from day to day and a double portion on the weekend. If there had been more grace than was needed, Israel would have stocked and piled it and decided they no longer needed the Lord.

Jesus taught us how to pray, and in His prayer, He said, "Give us our daily bread." Not tomorrow's bread, or enough to carry us until next year, but give us our "daily" bread.

If we are burdened by the presence of troubles that frustrate our Christian journey, we should hear the voice of God speaking to us, saying, "My grace is sufficient for thee!"

"My grace" can take the worst and turn it into the best!

"My grace" can take the least and turn it into the most!

"My grace" can take the lowest and turn it into the highest!

"My grace" can take a prison and turn it into a paradise!

"My grace" can take a shadow and turn it into sunshine!

"My grace" is sufficient for the lonely, no matter how pitiful they may seem!

"My grace" is sufficient for the weak, no matter how feeble their steps!

"My grace" is sufficient for the tired, no matter how exhausted their body!

"My grace" is sufficient for the soul, for it brings it to salvation.

"My grace" is sufficient for the heart, for it fills it with joy.

SEVEN-UPS

Scripture: "I will lift up mine eyes to the hills from whence cometh my help, My help cometh from the Lord who made the heaven and the earth" (Psalm 121:1–2).

INTRODUCTION

Our lives are filled with a variety of circumstances. Those that are positive and fulfilling we generally describe as our "ups." Those that are negative and unrewarding, we generally describe as our "downs."

We have found that life is filled with ups and downs. Good times and bad times. Successes and failures. We relish the "ups," and we dislike the "downs." The two are interconnected. The downs help us to appreciate the ups. The ups help us to bear the downs.

Every Christian should get consolation from knowing that the God we serve is one who stresses the "ups" of life and helps us to see the "downs" only as temporary lulls on the journey toward the Canaan land.

Are you feeling down today? Turn to God; he is on a higher plane!

Are you feeling sad today? Turn to God; he is on a happier level!

Are you feeling like a loser today? Turn to God; he will make you a winner.

As the steeple of every church points up, so does our faith point to God. In times of sadness, loneliness, or fear, all we need to remember is that God sits high and looks low and knows our every need!

- Turn to Jesus; he'll make everything all right!

–I–
Stand Up

The word "up" is an adverb that is used in conjunction with a verb to give it a clearer meaning. It generally indicates a higher elevation or plane. But there are at least seven adverbial applications for the word "up" that should be of interest to every Christian.

- The first of the seven adverbial uses for "up" is one that indicates that we should assume an upright position, is that we should *stand*.
- In Ephesians 6:13, Paul encouraged them to put on the whole armor of God so that they might be able to withstand the devil. He concluded the verse by saying, "Having done all to stand."
- It is the responsibility of every child of God to stand up for those things that are right and against those things that are wrong.

We must stand because we have a special encouragement to lift him up. The power of the cross is the source of salvation. The blood of Jesus can save us from sin.

When the hungry of the world crave the living bread, lift him up. He's the lily of the valley.

When the world thirsts for a cool drink of living water, lift him up. He's the bright morning star.

When the lost seek a source of atonement for sins, lift him up. He's the fairest of ten thousand.

I hear the songwriter say, "How to reach the masses, men of every birth, for the answer Jesus gave the key: And I, if I be lifted up from the earth, will draw all men unto men."

–VI–
When Time's Up, Move Up

The last two of the seven-ups refer to completely exhausting a supply and moving to a high plane. Acts 1:11 says, "Ye men of Galilee, why stand ye gazing into the heavens? The same Jesus, which is taken up from you into heaven, shall so come in like manner as ye have seen him go into heaven." When we have exhausted our time…here on earth, the Lord will tell us to move on up.

The signs all around us remind us that time is winding up. Jesus said, "When you hear of wars and rumors of wars, time is winding up." When you hear of famines and pestilences, time is winding up. When you hear of mothers against daughters and fathers against sons, time is winding up. Just a few more risings and fallings…and it will all be over down here.

But I hear Jesus say, "I go to prepare a place for you…come on up! The streets are paved with gold…come on up! It's always howdy and never goodbye…come on up!"

How Can the Ship Go Down When the Lord Is on Board?

Mark 4:37–40

 This is a striking picture. Let us consider what it reveals in Jesus. Firstly, it reveals natural weariness. Jesus had long hard days of toil. And the physical side of Jesus's life was subject to weariness, tiredness, and overexhaustion—just as any other man's life. Jesus was longing for quietness because the multitudes had constantly thronged him. He had no rest in the house. He had no rest in Judea. He had no rest in Samaria. He had no rest in Galilee. When he was resting on a well, there came a woman for water but had no rope.
 Peter's mother-in-law was sick with a fever and needed to be healed. Lazarus was dead and needed to be raised. Jesus saw the second multitudes. He selected the sea for quietness, and He commanded His disciples to pass over to the other side. The same day, He said, "Let us pass over to the other side." While Jesus was resting in the hindered

part of the ship on a pillow, a mighty storm arose (verses 35 and 36).

The sea in which the voyage occurred has some unusual accreditation, of which no other sea has. First of all, it is only forty miles long, eleven miles wide, and one hundred fifty feet deep. It is the only sea in the whole world that contains pure water, which you can drink, and it will not harm you. In the boundary of its forty miles, it also holds titles to names—the Sea of Tiberia, the Sea of Galilee, and the Gennesaret Lake.

Jesus was in the stern of the boat asleep, and there arose a mighty storm. The orioles were cracking. Water had filled the top deck. And they all were in jeopardy.

They went to Jesus, saying (verse 38) that their faith was gone. The storm signifies a condition of need in the hour of fear. We all need Jesus at all times. We need His brotherly care. We need His divine dignity. We need His perpetual presence. The churches need Him all over the world. God cares for you (1 Peter 5:7).

The disciples were upon Gennesaret Lake. Today, we are upon the sea of life in an uncertain world. The disciples took Jesus with them in the boat, and we have Him at all times with us (in the spirit.) David said (Psalm 139:7–8) (verse 39) that first of all, Jesus rebuked the wind, and the waves ceased. Secondly, He rebuked the disciples (verse 40), "How can the ship go down, with the Lord on board."

Jesus is putting the question to us today that he put to His disciples after He calmed the storm (verse 40) (theme).

"Don't you know the God that controls the element is on board? Don't you know God controls the atmosphere?

Don't you know, God controls the strongest beast. Don't you know, God controls the meanest man who ever trodded the globe of the universe. How can the ship go down with the Lord on board?" (Proverbs. 3:6).

Have you no faith? When we look at what Jesus is saying in sequence.

The second question answers the first question. Fear springs up where faith fails, for faith is one of the preventatives of fear. Fear runs from faith. Fear is not only agonizing and emotional. Pear paralyzes us. Fear humiliates and degrades every believer in God. Fear is the cause of the most awful wickedness.

In life, we have to learn how to really trust God. The general reason so many fail is they haven't yet learned how to trust Him.

To trust God, you will have to believe that He is able to turn failures into victories, small or large, high or low. (theme)

It is fear that has kept Europe and China armed for so many years (what a ruinous experience). Fear blocks the way of progress. Year after year, we are declaiming gross injustice to a system that permits grinding poverty to exist in the midst of prosperity. Those who stay down and out all of the time are afraid to stand up and step out on faith. Those who stay down and out all of the time are afraid to swing out and swim. They are not knowledgeable that God is on board. How can the ship go down with the Lord on board?

How can we fail with Jesus on board? Where is your faith? Where is your faith in tithe? Where is your faith that will assure you the claim of victories in Christ (verse 40)? Don't you know against any fear in the life of a Christian, there stands faith? Fear has always hindered the light and truth in the lives of God's people. Even in the church, in all ages (verse 38), fear has startled the churches. Fear has startled success in many marriages. Fear has broken up many homes; for any time there is no trust, there is no home.

What they were actually saying to Jesus was "Master, we are in a storm. And the ship is about to go down, and we can't swim. Master, what are you going to do about it? Master, do you really care? We have been with you all of this time. We left all to follow thee. Master, don't you care?"

You know, sometimes, we make the same insults to Jesus in the midst of our troubles. The minute it gets a little cloudy in many of our lives, most of us pray the same prayers. Where is your faith? Many times, we pray, "Master, we feel thrown away. It looks like nobody cares. It seems like nobody is on our side."

Don't you know the man that is on board? He is the man who scooped the seven seas with the palm of His hand. He caught the wind in His hand and declared (Isaiah 26:23). We can never enjoy this happy trust unless our mind stays on Jesus. The disciples of Jesus had seen his wonders. They had heard his teaching. Now they are companions of Jesus. Therefore, Jesus expected more than fear out of them (verse 40) (theme).

There are some concerns we are to give man. But we are to put our trust In god. Even if you are a welfare candidate, even if you have fallen into the valley of destitution, and even when the outlook of every aspect of life looks dreary and dark, put your trust in God. You can have anything in life you want and meet any obligation, but you need faith. You can have anything in life you desire if you learn to be faithful at your post of obligation to God (Psalm 32:9) (Psalm 145:16) (theme).

The storm that arose threatened the disciples' safety. We must learn from the history of this storm. As long as we are here in this life, we are going to be exposed to the tempest and trials of life. As long as we are here in this life, we are going to be exposed to doubts and dangers. And in the midst of all of our misfortune, it seems sometimes that Jesus is asleep. Sometimes, it seems like He has forsaken us. It seems sometimes like He has abandoned us. We must remember there has never been a time when God has forgotten His children. Therefore, faith in Jesus will abandon sorrows and despair (Hebrews 11:6).

This only tells us that on every voyage of life, storms will arise. Storms of failure will arise. Storms of falling will arise. Storms of losses will arise. Storms of confusion will arise. Storms of misfortune will arise. Storms of misunderstandings will arise. Storms of sickness and domestic will arise (in all of this.) We who have faith in him have no reason to be afraid because the Lord is on board. God told Moses when his faith got weak, one and a half miles from crossing the Red Sea (Exodus 14:13). The ship wouldn't go down when the Lord was on board. Many of us have to ask if the Lord is on board. Many of us have to ask the Lord as Peter did (Luke 17:5). The ship won't go down when the Lord is on board. The church will stand in the midst of the most dreadful storm (if the Lord is on board. Homes will remain unbroken if the Lord is on board (Matthew 16:18) (theme).

Never can we contemplate the character and saving might of Jesus without it renewing our faith. Jesus knew this was not an easy life because it was not an easy life with Him. Life is toilsome and wearisome. Sometimes, He wants us to realize our weaknesses and infirmities. Then have faith and trust in His promises. (theme)

Trust springs from confidence in the person you trust. Trust depends on the knowledge and confidence of another person. Faith may be great or small. Faith may be weak or strong. But trust in God has many degrees. There are many people who don't believe they can trust God for a single meal. Then there are others who can look to him without misgiving him to feed a thousand hungry mouths or convert a thousand sinners. (theme)

Our faith depends entirely on our knowing God. Therefore, faith will encourage us to base our prayers at their full face of worthwhile value. Then claim its fulfillment by a volitional act of faith. Man has no faith when his object is larger than his faith.

When one has lost confidence in himself and his fellow man, he may well have confidence in Jesus. When there is no exemption from dangers and temptation, still have faith in Jesus. When there is no exemption from sorrows and sin, still have faith in Jesus. If you need a million examples to justify your faith, you have no faith.

It only takes three things to justify us. These are faith, trust, and living Christlike. The absence of faith leaves the heart desolated and hopeless. Without faith in Jesus, we lose peace of mind. Without faith in Jesus, we lose strength for life. Without faith in Jesus, we cannot forgo the conflicts of life. Without faith in Jesus, we cannot endure suffering, age, or death. With faith, the ship will not go down. (theme)

Why are you so fearful? When Jesus is the same today, yesterday, and forever. It's a little harder to calm a troubling heart than it is to calm the sea. The sea can be calmed with one word from God. But it takes faith to calm a troubling heart. You can take a glass of water as long as your hand is not trembling. That water will be calm. But the minute you begin trembling, the water will begin to waver.

So it is with faith; as long as you have faith, you are not afraid. When doubt comes in, then you will fail. Faith makes you as calm as a serene child resting in his mother's arms. A little baby can sleep in this mother's bosom and expect no harm. When the thunder is clapping and the lightning is flashing and automobiles are backfiring, the baby has faith. In life, when troubles rise, in Jesus, you can rest in serene and calmness. (theme)

Psalm 105:1 says, "He cares for you."

You can take a wild bird out of the hedges, and his little heart will be throbbing for anxiety to rise on the pending of his wings because he has no faith. Then you can take a tamed bird out of the cage and hold it with that same hand. He will ride on his master's shoulder and sing sweet songs in his own language. So it is with faith. Where there is faith, fear flees. (theme)

On their voyage, it was cloudy. On the voyage, the wind got tempestuous. On the sea, it got dark; the ship began reeling and rocking. Peter was sitting at the wheel. The sea got rough. The water was coming in on the top deck. Peter held the wheel until veins rose up in his arms like ship cords. James said, "I think I'll go down and call the master."

Peter said, "No, James, let me go. I can tell him better than you." They went down and awakened him and said, "Master, we are in a storm. The water is coming from the inside."

Jesus rose up and said, "Peace be still."

The disciples asked, "What manner of man is this?" Even the wind and the waters obeyed him. The thundering hushed her murmuring. The lightning broke out in a smile and said, "We didn't mean no harm." (theme)

Jesus was still in the hinder part of the ship. He heard Daniel in the lion's den. He answered the Hebrew boys in the fiery furnace, "Call him." He was still saying, "Peace be still. Peace be still. Peace be still."

Whenever your storms rise in life, call the master. If it's trouble, call the master. If it's brokenheartedness, call the master. If it's some embarrassment, call the master. If it's sickness, call the master. If it's a weakness, call the master. If it's tears, call the master. We are in a storm. Can't you hear my Lord saying in your storm? Peace be still. After his death on the cross, he declared all power was in my hand. My peace I give, and my peace I'll leave with you.

PASSPORT TO HEAVEN

Scripture: "For God so loved the world that he gave his only begotten Son that whosoever believeth upon him should not perish but have everlasting life" (John 3:16).

INTRODUCTION

We usually think of passports in connection with travel from one country to another.

According to Webster, a passport is anything that can get you from one place to another or one state or condition to another.

In the secular world, we are bombarded with the idea of passports.

Education is generally flaunted as the "passport" to a good job. Education makes good jobs possible but does not always guarantee a job. Without an education, the best jobs are not possible.

An abundance of salable talents is also perceived as a "passport" to success. Those who have the gifts to sing, dance, or play musical instruments are said to have been born with the passports to succeed in their fingers.

Economists say that sound financial investments are the "passport" to financial security. They said the wise use of capital is the best insurance against poverty, but they don't tell us how to get the first funds to invest.

If a person wanted to make himself a place in the kingdom of God, what is his passport? What is it that can guarantee him a place in the kingdom?

There are some who believe that a passport into the kingdom of God is simply to join a church and find a place of service in the church program.

Ushering, for example, is a fine place of service. Ushers provide warm salutations for those who come to worship. They are the standard bearers of hospitality and the finest example of the true meaning of the word servant.

But simply serving as an usher is not a "passport" to heaven. Unfortunately, there are some who are uninformed but are not transformed by the renewing of their minds.

Simply looking good and marching down the aisles is not a "passport" to heaven. Unfortunately, there are some who are good at marching on the right foot, but their feet don't always walk up the king's highway.

Serving in the program is not a passport into the kingdom of God.

HOW CAN I ACQUIRE A PASSPORT?

How can one acquire a passport into the kingdom of God? If simply joining a church and serving in an auxiliary like the ushers or the choir is not sufficient, how can such a passport be obtained?

I MADE IT

Can this passport be obtained by the accumulation of riches? Can it be bought? This is what perplexed Solomon as he launched out on a pursuit of happiness. He accumulated untold riches and assembled for his use all the pleasure-providing vehicles of his time but concluded they all were vanity.

I heard Jesus speaking of the rich fool when he said, "What profit a man to gain the whole world and he loses his own soul?"

The passport that we are talking about cannot be bought by large contributions to the church that are not accompanied by even larger amounts of faith, repentance, and dedication to the cause of the kingdom.

This passport that we are talking about is not for sale.

Can this passport be obtained by quiet living? If I adopt a lifestyle that is what the diplomats describe as a "peaceful coexistence," that is, I don't bother anybody, and they don't bother me, won't that get me a passport into the kingdom of heaven?

This was the dilemma of the rich young ruler. He lived a good life. He didn't bother anybody, and he didn't break any laws. He felt his good living was enough to earn him a passport. But Jesus said there was one thing more he'd have to do, "Sell all he has, take up his cross, and follow me."

There are many people today who feel that simply living a quiet life of coexistence is enough to earn a passport. But just living a low-profile life of peace and tranquility will not get you a passport into the kingdom of God.

Can this passport be acquired by tagging along with another traveler? This was the dilemma faced by Elisha, who was followed closely by the prophet Elijah for many years. But when the chariot came down from heaven, Elisha found that it only had room for one. Elisha learned that although he could hold Elijah's mantle, he had to make his own mark and reserve his own place in the kingdom of God.

You can do some things in a crowd, but you have to talk to God by yourself.

You can hire people to do some things for you, but you have to talk to God for yourself.

Someone else can open doors for you, but you have to walk through the door of life for yourself.

You can hear the testimonies of others every day, but you have to try God for yourself.

Try him, and mountains shall become molehills.

Try him, and valleys shall be exalted.

ABOUT THAT PASSPORT

A passport bears the picture of the traveler and tells his identity.

If you are a heavenly traveler, your passport identifies you as a child of the king.

Every child of God can say without a doubt, "I know I am a child of God, although I move so slowly. I've been washed in the blood of the crucified lamb. I've been plunged beneath a fountain that flows from Immanuel's veins."

Not only does your passport tell who you are, but it tells where you come from.

— We've come through the rocky hills and valleys of destitution.

- We've come through the meandering peaks of hard times and survived the sweltering deserts of hopelessness.
- We've come climbing Jacob's ladder singing our new song, "I'm climbing up the rough side of the mountain, / holding on to God's unchanging hand."

Finally, a passport is no good unless it also has a seal. The seal notes that it is official, not fake, and backed up by the powers of the government.

Every heavenly traveler should know that his passport is:

- written with the pen of life
- his place of origin is listed as hard times and trouble
- his destination is listed as good times and happy days
- his nationality is listed as a child of the most high king
- his means of transportation is listed as a chariot that swings low

If anybody asks you who you are, tell them, "I'm a child of God."

- his passport is signed by the Holy Spirit
- it is written in the blood of the lamb, "I'm on my way to Canaan land!"

CERTIFICATES

Certificate of membership from the Hollywood Cathedral family. This is to certify that Elder Exie L. Smith has been accorded all the rights and privileges in the galaxy of this church, where everybody is a star, and Christ is the bright and morning star.

September 20, 2009, Hollywood Baptist Church Cathedral

The Full Gospel Baptist Church Fellowship of Suffolk County, New York.

To all whom this document comes greeting and salutation in the name of our Lord and Savior Jesus Christ, be it known that Exie L. Smith, Ordained Elder: Exie L. Smith, Full Gospel Baptist Church Fellowship of Suffolk County, New York.

Done this twenty-sixth day of September in the year of our Lord, 1994.

The Hofstra University, upon the recommendation of the faculty, has conferred upon Exie Lee Smith the degree of master's of science in education.

With all the rights and privileges pertaining thereto in witness whereof the seal of the university and signatures of its officers are hereunto affixed.

Given at Hempstead, New York, this first day of October, in the year of our Lord, 1900.

Suffolk County Executive Steven Bellone presents this certificate of appreciation to Elder Exie L. Smith in honor of her work that reflects the life and ideals of Dr. Martin Luther King Jr., Hollywood Full Gospel Baptist Cathedral.

New York State Assembly Citation Assemblywoman Kimberly Jean-Pierre—on behalf of the Assembly of the State of New York—is proud to present this citation to Elder Exie L. Smith on January 18, 2016.

It is incumbent upon myself to recognize the service of others such as yourself who selflessly provide for our community. Your efforts are highly recognized and truly embody the spirit and vision of Dr. Martin Luther King Jr.

Kimberly Jean-Pierre
11th District, NY

I MADE IT

Office of the Executive
(Citation)

Whereas, the County of Nassau is proud to recognize those outstanding individuals who made significant contributions to the enhancement of our region and the betterment of our residents and

Whereas, Elder Exie L. Smith is such an individual, and

Whereas, you, Elder Exie L. Smith, have worked diligently on behalf of causes and ideals which uphold the principles of human decency, and through the years, you have demonstrated a selfless commitment to the County of Nassau and its residents that warrants attention and gratitude, and

Whereas, the County of Nassau is proud to extend this commendation to you, Elder Exie L. Smith, as you are honored for your spirited leadership, dedication, and service to the community.

Now, therefore, I, Edward P. Mangano, Nassau County Executive, on this eighteenth day of January 2016, do hereby present this citation to:

Hollywood Full Gospel Baptist Cathedral Dr. Martin Luther King Jr.

Leadership Award presented to Elder Exie L. Smith

In honor of your work that reflects the Life and Ideals of Dr. Martin Luther King Jr.

January 18, 2016

Through the grace of God, I am still here. It has not been easy, but *I made it.*

God will do what He said He would do; no weapon formed against me shall prosper.

"I stood on God's Words."

New York Theological Seminary Elder Exie L. Smith, 1970, received her master's of divinity in New York, New York.

In appreciation for your outstanding service and dedication, Women of Excellence, May 9, 1990.

January 15, 1993, presented to Exie L. Smith in appreciation and untiring efforts on behalf of Dr. Martin Luther King Sagamore Children's Center.

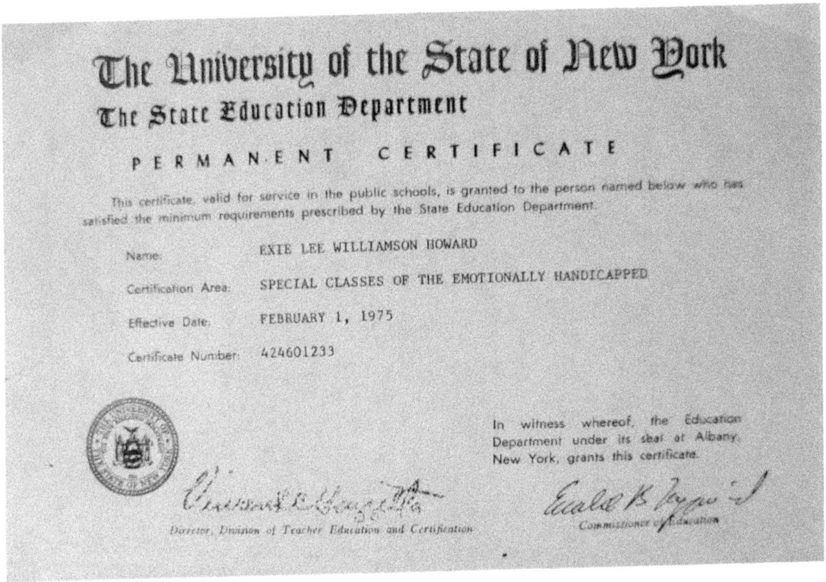

The University of the State of New York
The State Education Department

PERMANENT CERTIFICATE

This certificate, valid for service in the public schools, is granted to the person named below who has satisfied the minimum requirements prescribed by the State Education Department.

Name: EXIE LEE WILLIAMSON HOWARD

Certification Area: SPECIAL CLASSES OF THE EMOTIONALLY HANDICAPPED

Effective Date: FEBRUARY 1, 1975

Certificate Number: 424601233

In witness whereof, the Education Department under its seal at Albany, New York, grants this certificate.

Director, Division of Teacher Education and Certification

Commissioner of Education

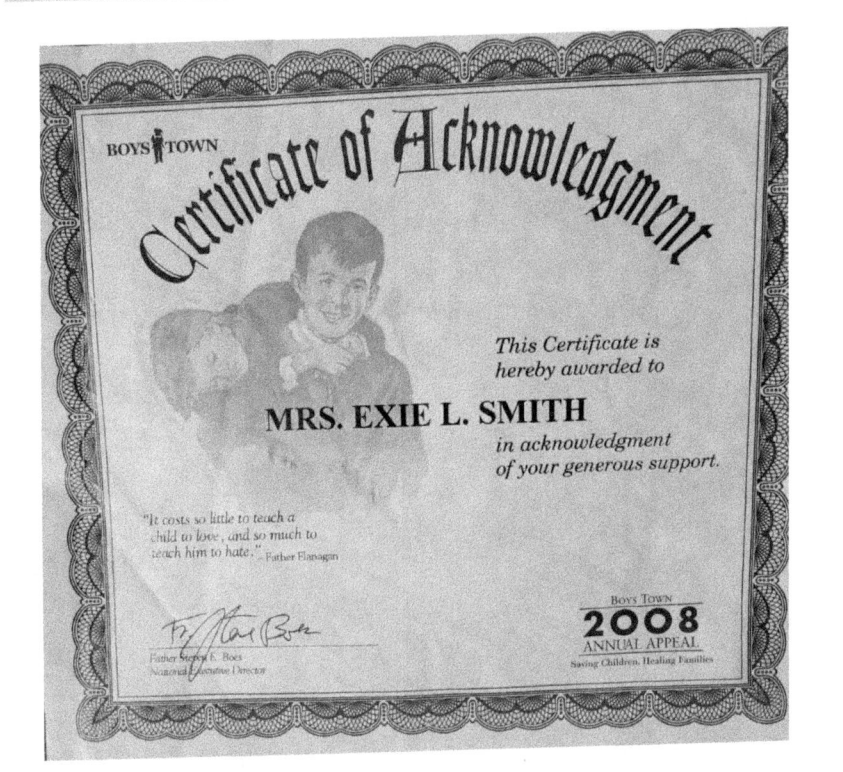

BOYS TOWN

Certificate of Acknowledgment

This Certificate is hereby awarded to

MRS. EXIE L. SMITH

in acknowledgment of your generous support.

"It costs so little to teach a child to love, and so much to teach him to hate." — Father Flanagan

Father Steven E. Boes
National Executive Director

BOYS TOWN
2008
ANNUAL APPEAL
Saving Children. Healing Families.

The University of the State of New York

The State Education Department

Public School Teacher Certificate

This certificate, valid for service in the public schools, is granted to the person named below who has satisfied the requirements prescribed by the State Education Department.

EXIE LEE WILLIAMSON HOWARD
12 SPRUCE ST.
NORTH AMITYVILLE, NY 11701

* Form: PERMANENT

Certificate number: 424601233

Certification area: SPECIAL EDUCATION

Effective date: SEPTEMBER 1, 1978

Given under the authority of the State Education Department

Director, Division of Teacher Education and Certification

Commissioner of Education

ALABAMA · STATE · COLLEGE

BY · AUTHORITY · OF · THE · STATE · BOARD · OF · EDUCATION · AND
ON · RECOMMENDATION · OF · THE · FACULTY
HEREBY · CONFERS · ON

EXIE · LEE · WILLIAMSON

THE · DEGREE · OF

BACHELOR · OF · SCIENCE · IN · ELEMENTARY · EDUCATION

WITH ALL THE HONORS RIGHTS PRIVILEGES AND RESPONSIBILITIES THEREUNTO APPERTAINING
IN · WITNESS · WHEREOF · THE · SEAL · OF · THE · COLLEGE · AND · THE · SIGNATURES · OF · THE
DULY · AUTHORIZED · OFFICERS · ARE · HEREUNTO · AFFIXED · AT · MONTGOMERY · ALABAMA
MAY · 25 · 1964

George C Wallace
GOVERNOR AND CHAIRMAN OF THE BOARD

PRESIDENT OF THE COLLEGE

G. R. Meadows
STATE SUPERINTENDENT OF EDUCATION
AND SECRETARY OF THE BOARD

About the Author

Exie L. Smith was born in Montgomery, Alabama, and she graduated from Alabama State University. She transitioned to New York. She graduated from Hofstra University in 1994 and received her master of science in education. She retired as a teacher for thirty-five years. She was called by God to teach and preach the gospel of Jesus Christ. She was ordained as an elder at the Hollywood Full Gospel Baptist Cathedral. She graduated from New York Theological Seminary and received a master of divinity degree.

Printed in the USA
CPSIA information can be obtained
at www.ICGtesting.com
LVHW021748120924
790643LV00013B/726